CHILD WELFARE TRAINING AND PRACTICE

CHILD WELFARE TRAINING AND PRACTICE

An Annotated Bibliography

Compiled by
John T. Pardeck,
Rebecca L. Hegar,
Kathy Newton Nance,
and
Cynthia Christy-Baker

Greenwood Press
Westport, Connecticut • London, England

Library of Congress Cataloging in Publication Data
Main entry under title:

Child welfare training and practice.

Includes indexes.
1. Social work with children—Study and teaching—Abstracts. 2. Social work education—Abstracts. 3. Child welfare—Abstracts. I. Pardeck, John T.
HV713.C3954 1982 362.7'07 82-11686
ISBN 0-313-23383-7 (lib. bdg.)

Library of Congress Catalog Card Number: 82-11686
ISBN: 0-313-23383-7

First published in 1982

Greenwood Press
A division of Congressional Information Service, Inc.
88 Post Road West, Westport, Connecticut 06881

Printed in the United States of America

10 9 8 7 6 5 4 3 2 1

CONTENTS

PREFACE

PURPOSE

The primary purpose of this annotated bibliography is to provide practitioners and educators working in the field of child welfare with information about readily available resource materials. Social workers in direct practice, supervision, administration, training, and education will be able to identify materials to enhance their knowledge and skills. In addition, students training for the field and new agency staff will be able to use the bibliography to become acquainted with many important works and resources for practice. Professionals in the fields of law, medicine, nursing, and education will also be able to use the bibliography in their practice.

Until the publication of this book of references and annotations, many of the available bibliographies concerning child welfare have been limited to specific topics such as child abuse. Some bibliographies have been aimed at general audiences, and even those annotated bibliographies designed specifically for child welfare training and education tend to focus primarily on traditional areas of practice leaving other important areas underdeveloped.

The authors, while preparing an earlier bibliography, searched for materials appropriate for training in child welfare and found that many materials have been produced about certain topics such as child abuse and neglect, assessment and interviewing, and foster care. However, the authors found few resources to be available for other aspects of training in child welfare.[1] One topic with particularly few training resources is practice with minority clients. The high number of minority group members within the child welfare system suggests that more should be available for trainers to help workers and other staff meet the special needs of these clients. This annotated bibliography lists the available training packages that deal with various ethnic groups. It also presents other materials that can be adapted for training social workers to serve child welfare clients from several racial and ethnic minorities.

This annotated bibliography is intended to draw together materials for training practice in the broad field of child welfare. It will also provide access to these materials not only for trainers, but also for educators, practitioners, and students who want to expand their knowledge and skills in this important field of social work.

COVERAGE AND SCOPE

The large majority of works referenced in the bibliography were published after 1964. However, several older classics have also been included. The general criterion that materials be published in 1965 or later ensures that the materials included, especially audiovisuals and training manuals, are available and current. The three general criteria established for the items are:

1) items developed after 1964, with a few exceptions;
2) readily available materials; and
3) materials appropriate for training in child welfare or useful to the educator, practitioner, or student for expanding knowledge and skills.

In most cases, works dealing primarily with research or social policy were omitted because such items are often not especially useful for training or for expanding practice skills.

The authors' original, extensive search for materials involved exploration of these main sources: computerized data bank, commercial and nonprofit publishers, and relevant government catalogs and social work journals. The search of social work journals included primarily *Child Welfare*, *Children Today*, *Journal of Social Work Education*, and *Social Work*. Universities and government agencies were found to have produced a large share of all of the available training materials.

ENTRIES

Citations of journal articles include authors, title, volume, year of publication, and inclusive pages. Book references include the author, title, edition cited, place of publication, publisher, date, and number of pages. For parts of large works, such as articles in books, authors and titles of the articles are usually given along with the full citation of the larger works.

Training manuals are listed by author, title, and place where materials can be ordered. The dates and number of pages of some training materials were unavailable.

Audiovisual materials, such as videotapes and films, include the author, title, and place where the material can be ordered. Most of the audiovisual entries give the date and the running time of the items. In some cases this information was not available.

The authors made concerted efforts to ensure that the materials cited in the bibliography were available. If there was uncertainty about the availability of an item, the publisher was contacted for information. Materials that are no longer available or that could not be verified were excluded.

ARRANGEMENT

The annotated items are arranged in seven sections by field of child welfare specialization or interest. These are: 1) Abuse and Neglect, 2) Law and the Court, 3) Substitute Care, 4) In-home Services and Parent Education, 5) Institutions and Special Needs Children, 6) Minority Clients, and 7) Training and Interviewing Methods.

The bibliographical entries are arranged within each section in alphabetical order. The items include journal articles, books, training manuals, audiovisual materials, and cassette tapes. With few exceptions, each item is listed only once, in the section to which it relates most closely.

INDEXES

The Author Index is a guide to the individuals or institutions that wrote or produced items which are cited in the bibliography. An Audiovisual Index helps the reader distinguish those items from other materials. The numbers following authors' names in the Author and Audiovisual Indexes refer to unique item numbers in the text of the bibliography.

The Subject Index serves two functions. It helps the user locate materials about a specific subject that falls within one of the seven major divisions (for example, the abuse and neglect materials concerning sexual abuse). It also allows the reader to identify entries about subjects that cut across the major sections (for example, materials about adolescents or single parents). Like the two other indexes, the subject index refers the reader to appropriate item numbers.

John T. Pardeck

NOTE

1. These findings are reported in "Analysis of an Exploration for Training Materials in Child Welfare," *Journal of Sociology and Social Welfare* 8 (1981): 841-846 by John T. Pardeck and Rebecca L. Hegar. A briefer report of the same search appears in a short note entitled "Training Materials in Child Welfare," *Journal of Continuing Social Work Education* 1, no. 2 (1981): 28, 35 by the same authors.

INTRODUCTION

Since the mid 1960s, child welfare practice has undergone numerous changes in the nature and scope of its services, legal mandate, and philosophy. The foster care population has increased, and this has led to renewed efforts to find permanent homes for children, to serve them more effectively in their own homes, and to develop early intervention programs. Ethnic minority children and others with special needs have gained increased professional attention, and rapid legal changes have also placed new demands on child welfare staff. Some of these recent developments in the child welfare field are reviewed here as an introduction to the literature that is included in the annotated bibliography.

After C. Henry Kempe introduced the concept and term "battered child syndrome" to the medical community in 1962, public awareness of the problems of child abuse and neglect grew.[1] Between 1963 and 1965, each state passed child abuse reporting laws, and the volume of reports to child protective agencies began to increase.[2] As more abusing and neglecting families became known to child protective agencies, the number of children entering foster care also increased.

Foster care has been a traditional way for society to meet the needs of children when their own families have serious problems. Alfred Kadushin reported in 1980 that the number of children in care, which had decreased dramatically after the Social Security Act was adopted in 1936, began to climb again during the 1960s. Between 1960 and 1972 the rate of placement of children increased by almost 75 percent.[3] This large increase in the foster care population was accompanied by major social work research studies into the causes, characteristics, and effects of child placement.

Findings from studies such as the Columbia University longitudinal study and Alan R. Gruber's study of Massachusetts foster children published in 1978, renewed professional concern about the length of time children spend in foster care. David Fanshel reported in 1979 that 48 percent of the New

York children who were placed because of abuse or neglect were still in placement at the end of the five-year study period.[4] In 1971, the average Massachusetts foster child had already been in the system for five years or longer, according to an extensive study by Gruber.[5]

The foster care research of the past decade also revealed what child welfare practitioners have long known: that a disproportionate share of the children who enter foster care come from poor and minority families. A national child welfare study reported in 1978 that 41 percent of U.S. foster children were black, Hispanic, Asian, or American Indian.[6] The philosophy of placement for minority children has shifted since the early 1960s. After a period of growing acceptance of cross-cultural placements, child welfare practitioners recognized that most foster children need foster families who share their own ethnicity. Contemporary placement practice stresses that "to the greatest extent possible, efforts should be made to preserve the foster child's religious, racial, and cultural heritage and to prevent discontinuities in values and cultural identity."[7]

Children with handicaps and others with special needs have also received increasing recognition within the child welfare system. Deinstitutionalization and the increased use of respite care, special day care, and placement in family settings are some of the trends.

The dramatic growth in the rate of placement and the findings of foster care research combine to reinforce the need to use services to prevent placement, except when protection from serious harm can be provided in no other way. There is a corresponding need to move children out of foster care and into permanent families more quickly.

Many of the demonstration projects and other new programs of the 1970s emphasized permanency planning and serving children and families in their own homes. Projects conducted in Oregon and in Alameda County, California both reported success in placing foster children in family settings which were planned to be permanent.[8] Comprehensive home-based services are among the approaches used to aid families who are having problems meeting the needs of their children. Efforts are also being made by professionals from several disciplines to design services to prevent serious parenting problems.[9]

Interdisciplinary concern about the problems of foster care has also brought about changes in the laws governing child protection and child placement.

The case of *In re Gault*, which required legal counsel for children in delinquency hearings, has also affected court procedures in child protective cases.[10] Some states have revised their laws to make it easier to free children for permanent placement, and others have increased the rights of foster parents.[11] Legal protection for the rights of parents is also changing. For example, the 1982 Supreme Court decision in *Santosky v. Kramer* requires the use of a stricter standard of proof, "clear and convincing" evidence, in hearings to establish lack of parental fitness and to make termination of parental rights possible.[12]

All of these developments in the field of child welfare combine to place increased demands on staff for: investigative and legal expertise, ethnic-sensitive practice, ability to engage and work with the parents of children in foster care, and skill in preventing and in limiting the length of placement. The definition of child welfare services that appears in the Child Welfare Act of 1980 reflects this broad range of services and clients:

> Child welfare services means public social services which are directed toward the accomplishment of the following purposes: (1) protecting and promoting the welfare of all children, including handicapped, homeless, dependent, or neglected children; (b) preventing or remedying, or assisting in the solution of problems which may result in the neglect, abuse, exploitation, or delinquency of children; (c) preventing the unnecessary separation of children from their families by identifying family problems, assisting families in resolving their problems, and preventing breakup of the family where the prevention of child removal is desirable and possible; (d) restoring to their families children who have been removed, by the provision of services to the child and the families; (e) placing children in suitable adoptive homes, in cases where restoration to the biological family is not possible or appropriate; and (f) assuring adequate care of children away from their homes, in cases where the child cannot be returned home or cannot be placed for adoption.[13]

This expanded definition places greater emphasis on preventive services and on service to handicapped children and juvenile delinquents. While it represents a change from other recent definitions in federal law, it indicates a return to the concept of promoting the welfare of all children.

This annotated bibliography reflects the recent trends in child welfare practice and the new federal definition. It includes material about services to handicapped and delinquent children, as well as to neglected and abused children. It encompasses preventive services, particularly parent education, in addition to services to children in their own homes and in substitute care. Legal issues and court work are the subjects of one section, while another focuses on services to ethnic minorities. The final section includes materials about training staff and volunteers and assessing and interviewing clients.

The rapid development of the child welfare field has been paralleled by a great expansion in the child welfare literature: new journals, comprehensive and specialized texts, and a wealth of audiovisual materials. This annotated bibliography is a basic guide to the literature that is designed to prepare and train practitioners for the changing field of child welfare.

Rebecca L. Hegar

NOTES

1. C. Henry Kempe et al., "The Battered Child Syndrome," *Journal of the American Medical Association* 181 (1962): 17-24.

2. Vincent De Francis and Carroll L. Lucht, *Child Abuse Legislation in the 1970's*, revised ed. (Denver: American Humane Association, 1974), p. 6.

3. Alfred Kadushin, *Child Welfare Services*, 3d ed. (New York: MacMillan, 1980), p. 321.

4. David Fanshel, "Status Changes of Children in Foster Care: Final Results of the Columbia University Longitudinal Study," *Child Welfare* 55 (1979): 149.

5. Alan R. Gruber, *Children in Foster Care: Destitute, Neglected . . . Betrayed* (New York: Human Sciences Press, 1978), p. 39.

6. Ann Shyne and Anita G. Schroeder, *National Study of Social Services to Children and Their Families* (Washington, DC: U.S. Children's Bureau, DHHS, 1978), p. 30.

7. Charles Horejsi, *Foster Family Care* (Springfield, IL: Charles C. Thomas, 1979), p. 176.

8. Arthur Emlen et al., *Overcoming Barriers to Planning for Children in Foster Care* (Washington, DC: U.S. Children's Bureau, DHHS, 1978); Theodore Stein, Eileen D. Gambrill, and Kermit Wiltse, *Children in Foster Homes: Achieving Continuity of Care* (New York: Praeger Publishing Co., 1978).

9. Sheila Maybanks and Marvin Bryce, *Home-Based Services for Children and Families: Policy, Practice and Research* (Springfield, IL: Charles C. Thomas, 1979); Mario D. Fantini and Rene Cardenes, editors, *Parenting in a Multi-Cultural Society* (New York: Longman, 1980).

10. In re Gault, 387 U.S. 1 (1967); Patrick R. Tamilia, "Neglect Proceedings and the Conflict Between Law and Social Work," *Duquesne Law Review* 9 (1971): 588.

11. Roberta Gottesman, *The Child and the Law* (St. Paul, MN: West Publishing Co., 1981), p. 116; Joseph P. Carrieri, *The Foster Child: From Abandonment to Adoption* (New York: Practicing Law Institute, 1977), p. 325.

12. *Santosky v. Kramer*, 50 *Law Week* 4333 (1982).

13. Public Law 96-272, Section 103 (Child Welfare Act of 1980).

ACKNOWLEDGMENTS

The authors thank Dr. Margaret M. Campbell, who first noted the need for an annotated child welfare bibliography, and other colleagues at Tulane University for their moral support and suggestions. Sincere thanks go also to Colleen Plaisted for typing the final manuscript and to Roxy Wright for other typing and assistance. Jean Pardeck's help with editing is also appreciated. Finally, special thanks go to Paul Kobasa of Greenwood Press for his assistance throughout the project.

John T. Pardeck, Ph.D.
Rebecca L. Hegar, MSSW
Kathy N. Nance, MSSW
Cynthia Christy-Baker, MSW

April 1982

CHILD WELFARE TRAINING AND PRACTICE

1

ABUSE AND NEGLECT

1. Abel, C.M. Medical, Legal and Training Aspects of Child Abuse and Neglect: A Springboard for Discussion. Washington, DC: U.S. Printing Office, Office of Child Development, Publication CD - 02465, n.d. 75 pages.

   This is a catalogue of video tape modules designed as training aides to enhance the response of professionals to the problems of child abuse and neglect.

2. Academy of Health Sciences, U.S. Army, Merry Go Round (Videocassette). Washington, DC: U.S. Department of the Army, Training Division, 1978. 44 minutes.

   This was developed for military personnel, parents, social workers and the general public. The videocassette shows several causes of child abuse and the family situations that led to the abuse. A multidisciplinary team approach with focus on counseling, parenting, training and education in helping abusive parents is given.

3. Adamowicz, D., ed. Child Abuse and Neglect, The Problem and its Management: An Overview of the Problem, vol. 1. Washington, DC: U.S. Government Printing Office, 1975. 63 pages.

   This first volume of a three part series is appropriate for training a general audience. It covers the origin, development, and expression of abusive and neglectful behavior. General characteristics of maltreated children are listed. Two alternative approaches to the case management of child abuse are discussed.

4. Adamowicz, D., ed. Child Abuse and Neglect, The Problem and its Management: The Roles and Responsibilities of Professionals, vol. 2. Washington, DC: U.S. Government Printing Office, 1975. 89 pages.

The second in a three part series, this volume is directed to professionals in social services. It addresses the roles and responsibilities of professionals in dealing with parents' rights and children's rights. The worker's attitudes and feelings are addressed. The use of the multidisciplinary team is also covered.

5. Adamowicz, D., ed. Child Abuse and Neglect, The Problem and its Management: Community Team, An Approach to Case Management and Prevention, vol. 3. Washington, DC: U.S. Government Printing Office, 1975. 208 pages.

The third volume in a three part series may be used for training the community in the use of multidisciplinary diagnostic treatment. and preventive programs for abusive and neglectful families.

6. AIMS Industrial Media Services, Inc. Child Abuse and the Police (Film). 626 Justin Avenue, Glendale, CA 91201, 1973. 30 minutes.

The film was developed for training law enforcement officers. It shows a family's involvement with the police and the law in a child abuse case. It demonstrates how doctors and police determine that a child's injuries are the result of abuse.

7. American Human Association, Children's Division. Teaching Record in Child Protective Services. The Masterson Case. Neglected Children--Constructive Use of the Juvenile Court. P.O. Box 1266, Denver, CO 80701, n.d. 33 pages.

This material is for use primarily by persons providing services to the neglecting family. It is a case record depicting the circumstances surrounding a welfare mother who is unable to care adequately for her teenage sons. Casework combined with effective utilization of community resources is demonstrated. Chronic truancy, inadequate clothing, and inadequate parenting were observed by child protective service representatives. The eventual placement of the children on supervisory probation by the juvenile court and juvenile counseling by a psychiatrist has contributed to an improvement in attitudes and effort toward more constructive lives.

8. American Humane Association on Children's Division. Teaching Record in Child Protective Services. The Nancy Smith Case. Nelgected Child--Unmarried Mother. P.O. Box 1266, Denver, CO 80701, n.d. 11 pages.

This material was developed for social service providers and is an actual case record illustrating the protective service techniques used in helping a physically and emotionally neglected child, who was born out of wedlock. The young, deprived mother was unable to maintain a stable family relationship. The caseworker was able to make the circumstances of the case clear to the mother by analyzing the mother's concepts of life; as a result, the mother agreed to have her child placed for adoption.

9. Boyne, Linda. Failure to Thrive: The Child Who Hasn't Blossomed. Columbus, OH: Child Abuse Project Social Service Department, Children's Hospital, 1979. 40 pages.

This was developed for protective service workers and public health nurses. It may be used to assist in the identification of infants and children at risk for neglect and/or failure to thrive. Normal growth and development guidelines are presented with appropriate feeding practices for children of various ages. Procedures to follow are given once neglect or failure to thrive are identified.

10. Cavalcade Productions. Barb: Breaking the Cycle of Abuse (Film). P.O. Box 1182, Washington, DC 20013: National Center on Child Abuse and Neglect, 1977. 28 minutes.

The film is a revised version of "Don't Give Up On Me." Increased emphasis is placed on the abusive mother, her feelings toward her children, and her guilt feelings. New sequences deal with a weekend self-help therapy group in which Barb participates. The film ends with a statement by a lay person who participated in the film, regarding her initial feelings toward abusive parents and the insight she gained into the personal problems that may lead to abuse.

11. Cornell University, Family Life Development Center. Child Abuse: A Total Treatment Perspective (Videocassette or Videotape). MVR Hall, Ithaca, NY: Cornell Television Center, 1976. 28 minutes.

A simulation of the third meeting between the child abuse team of Onondaga County, NY and parents whose child has been removed from home is presented. A team treatment approach is used, which includes a child protective service worker, a psychiatrist, a public health nurse, and a parent aide. Efforts are made to resolve the couple's problems, which include the stepfather's inability to find employment, the mother's

(Cornell University)

transportation problems, and interpersonal problems with the child. Emphasis is placed on the importance of the parents' involvement with the team. Their presence holds both the family and the professionals accountable for their participation in the total treatment plan. A discussion guide is available.

12. Helfer, Ray E. A Self-Instructional Audiovisual Program on Child Abuse and Neglect (Filmstrips, Audiocassetts and Workbooks). National Center for Child Abuse and Neglect, Community Office of Child Development, P.O. Box 1182, Washington, DC: Children's Bureau, 1974. 30 minutes each unit.

Unit I, "The World of Abnormal Rearing," discusses poor or abnormal parenting. Objectives of this unit are to diagram and discuss the abnormal child-rearing cycle and to demonstrate the abnormal spin-offs of the cycle.

In Unit II, "Making the Diagnosis of Abuse and Neglect in Small Children," a pediatrician covers information that must be known before a diagnosis of abuse or neglect can be made. The primary objective is to demonstrate the need for understanding the basic psychodynamics of child battering in order to develop a therapeutic program. It also reviews criteria for diagnosis.

Unit III, "The Diagnostic Process," covers the steps which should be taken in developing a diagnosis and treatment plan for the families of abused children. The accompanying workbook contains a diagram of community and medical facilities. A flowchart of specific steps leading to diagnosis and treatment is gradually developed with the use of a diagram.

Unit IV, "Current Therapeutic Programs," discusses two major areas: 1) the theoretical basis for unsuccessful treatment programs, and 2) the ways of determining if a home is safe for a given child. It presents six major points of treatment.

Unit V, "Developing Community Programs," presents information which can be used in developing a multidisciplinary diagnostic treatment and preventive program for families and children facing the problem of child abuse and/or neglect. It provides a definition of community and discusses how the volume of child abuse cases and child abuse services is affected by the community. The film describes which professionals make up the professional team, their roles, and the kinds of programs which might be developed. Included is a summary of the four major areas covered.

(Helfer, Ray E.)

Unit VI, "Review and Preview," is a summary review of the information in Units 1-5. It includes a brief description of the two methods of case review and treatment of families, the Pascal method and the Kissinger method. The unit concludes with speculations about the future of the child abuse and neglect field.

13. Helfer, Ray E., and Kempe, Henry C., eds. Child Abuse and Neglect: The Family and the Community. Cambridge, MA: Ballinger Publishing Co., 1976. 460 pages.

This book focuses on the dynamics of the abusive environment and on how effective treatment programs can be developed and implemented. The material provides information on the management of child abuse.

14. Helfer, Ray E., and Kempe, Henry C., eds. Battered Child 2d ed. Chicago: University of Chicago Press, 1974. 262 pages.

This is an encyclopedia type volume covering the historical, medical, psychiatric, social and legal aspects of child abuse. The roles of the social worker, physician, and law enforcement officer are discussed. Chapters also include radiological aspects of the battered child syndrome, and the pathology of child abuse.

15. Human Relations Media. Violence in the Family: Four-Part Program (Filmstrips with Record of Cassette Sound). Same-Day Service Department, 175 Tompkins Avenue, Pleasantville, NY 10570, 1979.

Part 1, "Dynamics of Family Violence," studies the many reasons for violence in American families. Part 2, "Child Abuse and Neglect," explains the prevalence of child abuse and punishment. It probes the motivations of abusive, neglectful parents and their effects on the growing child. Part 3, "Battered Wives," explores causes of wife beating and the deep historical roots of violence against women. Part 4, "Adolescent Abuse," studies the widespread incidence of adolescent abuse and its effects on teenage victims. Sensitive case studies describe the conflicts and personality disturbances that lead to adolescent abuse. It discusses possible solutions to family violence.

16. Jefferson, C.A., ed. Training Manual. Washington, DC: Howard University Institute for Urban Affairs and Research, 1976. 287 pages.

This is a 7-part comprehensive child abuse and neglect training manual and was developed for use by state welfare agencies in Federal Region III. The manual contains units on social values clarification, the

(Jefferson, C. A.)

dynamics of abusive parents, legal aspects, crisis intervention, investigation, and treatment. Selected readings for educators and nurses are included along with a glossary of technical terms encountered in the abuse and neglect field. Extensive use of case reports, special questionnaires and role models is made.

17. Jones, Barbara McComb; Tenstrom, Linda L.; MacFarlane, Kee, eds. Sexual Abuse of Children: Selected Readings. Washington, DC: National Center on Child Abuse and Neglect, Children's Bureau, DHHS, 1980. 193 pages.

This is a book of selected readings which present material on etiology and short-term management of sexual abuse with sections that deal specifically with incest, treatment and interviewing techniques and sexual exploitation of children for commercial purposes.

18. Justice, Blair, and Justice, Rita. The Broken Taboo. New York, NY: Human Sciences Press, 1979. 304 pages.

This is a scientific report on incest: who commits it, why it occurs, what the consequences are, and what can be done about the problem. It presents the typical personality structures of the kinds of parents most likely to commit incest, the reactions of the children and the short and long-term effects on them. Other areas covered are the influence of contemporary morality in fostering the growing frequency of incest and the relationship between the breakdown of traditional social structures and incest.

19. Kallisch, Beatrice J. Child Abuse and Neglect: An Annotated Bibliography. Westport, CT: Greenwood Press, 1978. 535 pages.

This is an annotated bibliography designed for use in training, classroom teaching and development of curriculum modules.

20. Kempe, Henry C., and Helfer, Ray E., eds. Helping the Battered Child and His Family. Philadelphia, PA: Lippincott, 1972. 313 pages.

This book focuses on helping families of battered children. Chapters are written by a social worker, nurse, psychiatrist, policeman, judge, lawyer and psychologist. The program description may be used to institute or develop new programs.

21. Martin, Harold P., ed. The Abused Child: A Multi-Disciplinary Approach to Developmental Issues and Treatment. Cambridge, MA: Ballinger Publishing Co., 1976. 336 pages.

For use by trainers and practitioners, this material focuses on the consequences of abuse and on how the abused child's cognitive, emotional and social development needs can be met. It gives a variety of issues to be considered in the prediction of abuse and neglect.

22. Meckes, R. E. Training Curriculum for Lay Therapists. Philadelphia, PA: St. Christopher's Hospital for Children, 1975. 26 pages.

This is a training curriculum for lay therapists. It is designed to give the roles and responsibilities of lay therapists and to develop skills in dealing with abused children and their families.

23. Media Marketing W-STAD. Cipher in the Snow (Film). Provo, UT 84602, Brigham Young University, 1973. 24 minutes.

This film for the general public is the true story of a boy no one thought was important until his sudden death one snowy morning. This is a dramatization of psychological abuse.

24. Mike Williams Associates. Acute Phase: Consulting Pediatrician (Film). 329A 17th Street, Box 564, Manhattan Beach, CA 90266, 1974. 20 minutes.

This film was developed for case work staff and demonstrates the role of the pediatric consultant in a child abuse case. It covers aspects of data gathering for a diagnosis, determining the safety of the home and development of a long-term treatment program.

25. Mike Williams Associates. Diagnosing Child Abuse and Neglect Via Physical Findings (Slide series with cassette tapes). Box 564, Manhattan Beach, CA 90255, n.d.

This slide series is directed to professionals involved in making a child abuse and neglect diagnosis. The presentation consists of slides with physical descriptions of the results of various types of abuse, including burns, bruises, bone injuries and failure to thrive.

26. Minnesota State Department of Public Welfare and Minnesota University Center for Urban and Regional Affairs. Like a Motherless Child. Toward Understanding Neglecting Parents (Filmstrip - audio cassette). 658 Cedar, St. Paul, MN 55155, 1976. 12 minutes.

This is a dramatization of an interview between a family service worker and a neglectful mother. It focuses on the development of a positive worker-client relationship. The social service worker explains that the children were removed from the mother's custody because of apparent poor child care practices. As the conversation progresses, visual close-ups of the individuals show the range of sentiments exhibited by the mother in reaction to interview topcis; during the interview she moves from a position characterized by defensiveness and anger to stages of self-examination and shame, culminating in a final acceptance of the facts and a willingness to receive help. A discussion guide is included.

27. Minnesota State Department of Public Welfare and Minnesota University Center for Urban and Regional Affairs. The Theft of Childhood. Toward Understanding Abusive Parents (Filmstrip - audio cassette). 658 Cedar, St. Paul, MN 51555, n.d. 15 minutes.

This story of an abusive father, from infancy to parenthood, follows introductory statements written by Dr. Brandt Steele (National Center for the Prevention and Treatment of Child Abuse and Neglect, Denver). Dr. Steele emphasizes the cyclical, generational aspects of inadequate mothering. The photographic dramatization illustrates several aspects of this phenomenon. An infant is born to an unwed mother who was abused herself. The mother perceives the child as an object to meet her needs and only meets his needs when they are convenient to her; the infant is, thus, fed and cleaned according to her own whims. As a toddler, the child is perceived as depriving the mother or acting against her. The child is punished and abused for small incidents. As a result of this inconsistency and lack of trust on the part of the mother, the child develops feelings of inadequacy. The child became withdrawn and could not develop new relationships.

28. Missouri University Academic Support Center. Child Abuse Education and Training Program (Videocassette). 505 East Stewart Road, Columbia, MO 65201: University of Missouri Film Library, n.d.

The problem of child abuse and neglect in Missouri is overviewed. Information is provided on the role of the social worker; juvenile court hearings; criminal court procedures; proper testimony by the social service worker; reactions of workers, parents and the public

(Missouri University)

to the problem; and methods of developing awareness of the extent of the problem in schools and communities. Common myths surrounding the abusive parent are dispelled, and the need to recognize the signs of abuse, and the treatment rather than punishment of the abusive parent is stressed. Sections of Missouri law are cited and dramatizations of case investigation, court hearings, and developing community awareness are included.

29. MTI Teleprograms, Inc. Child Abuse: Cradle of Violence (Film). 3710 Commercial Avenue, Northbrook, IL 60062, 1981. 20 minutes.

This is a film for use by practitioners and the general public. It focuses on the preventive aspects of child abuse. Parents who have been abusers and received help are interviewed and share experiences. Several reasons for abuse such as frustration, stress and guilt feelings are revealed. Methods for reporting abuse by community members are given.

30. MTI Teleprograms, Inc. Child Abuse: Police Intervention (Film). 3710 Commercial Avenue, Northbrook, IL 60062, 1982. 26 minutes.

This film deals with the role of the law enforcement officer in handling child abuse and neglect. Three dramatizations are presented to demonstrate situations confronted by law enforcement officers.

31. MTI Teleprograms, Inc. Don't Give Up On Me (Film). 3710 Commercial Avenue, Northbrook, IL 60062, 1980. 28-1/2 minutes.

This material illustrates for social workers the problem solving process involved in the case of a suspected child abuser. The main character is viewed in her home, with her caseworker, at group meetings, at a meeting with her ex-husband, and in the courtroom. Each of the scenes in the film involves her interacting with various persons from the time she is accused of abuse by a neighbor until she has joined a self-help group composed of child abusers and counselors. Here she reveals her need for affection, her fears and the fact that her behavior toward her child is much like her mother's behavior toward her.

32. MTI Teleprograms, Inc. Double Jeopardy (Film). 3710 Commercial Avenue, Northbrook, IL 60062, 1981. 40 minutes.

Developed for social workers, this film deals with the recognition of the needs and fears of the abused child.

(MTI Teleprograms, Inc.)

Attention is paid to the abused child's developmental level. This series of vignettes demonstrates negative and positive interactions between sexually assaulted children, the criminal justice system and social service personnel. Actual case histories are provided by social workers, child advocates, police detectives, pediatricians and prosecuting attorneys.

33. MTI Teleprograms, Inc. Incest: The Victim Nobody Believes (Film). 3710 Commercial Avenue, Northbrook, IL 60062, 1981. 20 minutes.

Developed for training the general public, this film discusses the issues of sexual abuse. Material is directed at depicting the extent of sexual child abuse and points out the impact a childhood incestuous experience has on the victim's life. Three young women discuss factors of fear, confusion, isolation and guilt associated with experiences of sexual abuse.

34. MTI Teleprograms, Inc. Ordinary People (Film). 3710 Commercial Avenue, Northbrook, IL 60062, 1982. 25 minutes.

This film is directed to social service professionals, trainers and the general public. The film demonstrates how "ordinary people" can be child abusers. Danger signals in a normal family are indicated throughout the film. The potential for violence accompanied by a variety of distress signals is demonstrated.

35. MTI Teleprograms, Inc. The Last Taboo (Film). 3710 Commercial Avenue, Northbrook, IL 60062, 1980. 28 minutes.

This was developed for training a public audience and professional staff. Actual victims of incest describe their experiences and traumas. It was filmed during a workshop and demonstrates the process of facilitating a self-healing experience. The workshop involves women who have years of repression and inadequate adjustment to traumatic incidents that occurred.

36. MTI Teleprograms, Inc. The Sexually Abused Child: Identification/Interview (Film). 3710 Commercial Avenue, Northbrook, IL 60062, 1981. 10 minutes.

This film was developed for training of teachers and guidance counselors. It demonstrates the technique needed to effectively interview the abused child without further traumatizing the child. The film examines methods of establishing rapport, ways to deal with protective feelings toward the abuser and interpretation and use of non-verbal information.

37. Naki, B. Dynamics of Child Abuse and Neglect. Instructor's Training Manual. Honolulu, HI: Hawaii Family Stress Center, 1976. 192 pages.

This manual contains 5 teaching units which describe the profile of the abusive parent, differentially characterize the abused from the normal child, identify community resources which are useful to abusive families and describe the role of the helping person in abuse and neglect cases. The manual was designed for a 7-week training program presented in a seminar-lecture format, utilizing audiovisual materials and guest lecturers from the community. An assessment test for each of the 5 major units of the course is incorporated to follow the progress of the student. Selected reading material, case study presentations and role plays are utilized.

38. National Center on Child Abuse and Neglect. Identifying Neglect: Before It's Too Late (Filmstrip-audiocassette). General Services Administration, Order Section, Washington, DC 20409: National Audiovisual Center, n.d. 12 minutes.

Child neglect is defined and various signs of neglect are depicted. In general, a neglect situation is indicated by threats to the child's health and refusal of assistance by the parents or caretakers. Typical signs of child neglect include abandonment, lack of preventive health care, inadequate and unclean clothing, inadequate supervision (especially of infants), the failure to thrive syndrome, poor parent-child relations and unsafe shelter. The problem occurs at all income levels and cultural differences must be taken into account when assessing a possible neglect situation.

39. National Center on Child Abuse and Neglect. Investigating Report of Child Abuse and Neglect (Film). General Services Administration, Order Section, Washington, DC 20309: National Audiovisual Center, 1976. 28 minutes.

Separate cases of child abuse and neglect are depicted. The dramatization of the abuse case shows the physician's diagnosis, an interview with the mother and involvement by child protective service authorities. The second dramatization concerns the role of police in investigating a report of children left unsupervised.

40. National Center on Child Abuse and Neglect. Physical Abuse: What Behavior Can Tell Us (Filmstrip, audiocassette). General Services Administration, Order Section, Washington, DC 20409: National Audiovisual Center, n.d. 14 minutes.

Behavioral signs of child abuse are depicted and described, including introversion, extreme passivity, shyness and fearfulness. The less severely abused child is often frustrated by his parents' inconsistent behavior, and may be aggressive and hyperactive; acting out is common. Many children exhibit both types of behavior; extreme behavior should be noted. Characteristics of abusive parents include tenseness, apathy, displeasure with the child, and dependence on the child.

41. National Center on Child Abuse and Neglect. Physical Indicators of Abuse and Signs of Alert (Filmstrip - audiocassette). General Services Administration, Order Section, Washington, DC 20409: National Audiovisual Center, 1976. 13 minutes.

This filmstrip presents photographs, x-rays and illustrations of common injuries found in physically abused children. Bruises, burns, abrasions, lacerations, metaphyseal and spiral fractures, epiphyseal separation, periosteal inflammation, subdural and retinal hematomas, and internal injuries which result from strong blows and kicks are described and depicted. Frequently in cases of physical abuse, the parents offer inadequate explanation for the injuries.

42. National Center on Child Abuse and Neglect. Sexual Abuse: The Family (Film). General Services Administration, Order Section, Washington, DC 20409: National Audiovisual Center, 1976. 25 minutes.

This film gives an overview of intrafamily sexual abuse of children and includes definitions of the problem, common myths, physical and behavioral indicators, family dynamics, and different approaches to the problem. Raylene Devine (Children's Hospital Medical Center, Washington, DC), Henry Giaretto (Santa Clara County Sexual Abuse Program, San Jose, CA), and Betty Stovall (Detroit Children's Aid Society) discuss the problem and their approaches to it. Family conservation is the primary treatment goal. A simulated demonstration of proper interviewing techniques with those involved in a sexual abuse case is presented with emphasis on minimizing the trauma for the child.

43. National Center on Child Abuse and Neglect. User Manual Series. Washington, DC: U.S. Government Printing Office, 1978.

These materials include a series of handbooks developed for social workers and community personnel. The series includes: The Role of the Mental Health Professional which focuses on the prevention and treatment of abuse; Treatment for Abused and Neglected Children which presents the needs of the abused and neglected child with some practical ideals and explanations for intervention; and Child Protective Services: A Guide For Workers which deals with how to develop a child protective service delivery system.

44. National Center on Child Abuse and Neglect. We Can Help. A Curriculum on the Identification, Reporting, Referral and Case Management of Child Abuse and Neglect (Multi-media). P.O. Box 1182, Washington, DC 20013: DHHS, 1976.

This comprehensive course of study on child abuse and neglect consists of a 12-unit core curriculum for single group or multidisciplinary training audiences, and a 4-unit specialized curriculum for social workers, medical and health professionals, educators, and law enforcement professionals. The core curriculum is designed to last approximately 35 hours and consists of 2 sequences, the identification sequence and the community response sequence. The identification units examine each type of maltreatment; the social, familial, and personal factors that contribute to abuse and neglect; and various legal and operational definitions that promote identification. The community response units examine procedures for responding to suspected cases of child abuse and neglect. The roles of various community agencies, including the courts, are explored. Attitudes and feelings of the trainees and the various groups that become involved are also examined in both sequences. Each specialized curriculum unit may be used independently and was designed to train professionals in the particular skills required in their field to identify, report, refer and manage cases of child abuse and neglect. Each unit in both parts of the curriculum consists of a manual for the trainer that describes or provides all the necessary elements to conduct the unit. Objectives are outlined throughout the curriculum. These and the entire curriculum are listed and described in an introductory booklet to the trainer's manual.

45. National Education Television and Radio Center. The Battered Child (Motion Picture). Indiana University, Audio-Visual Center, Bloomington, ID 47401, 1969. 68 minutes.

Based on the book entitled The Battered Child by Henry C. Kempe and Ray E. Helfer, this is a documentary study of child abuse and neglect. It shows a team of doctors and social workers at the University of Colorado Medical Center working with actual cases of abuse and neglect. Focus is on the causes of physical abuse and treatment of children affected mentally.

46. National Institute of Mental Health. Borderline Case: Initial Conference; Conference Part II, Home Visit; Conference Part III, Follow-up (Film). 5600 Fishers Lane, Rockville, MD 20852, 1976. 30 minutes, 14 minutes, 11 minutes respectively.

Initial Conference: Group involvement in the management of a child abuse and neglect case is depicted. The group, which consists of a teacher, social worker, physician, and public health nurse, responded to a teacher's report of suspected child battering. Causative factors of abuse are reviewed. The roles of the public health nurse and social worker in formulating a case of management plan aimed at preserving the family are noted.

Part II Home Visit: A home visit by a teacher and social worker is depicted, in which the reason for the suspected abuse report are explained to the parents. The results of a multidisciplinary team meeting concerning the case are reviewed for the parents, stressing the need for counseling and self-help. The mother is encouraged to express her feelings. The sound track quality of the film is fair.

Part III Follow-up: The follow-up session of a child abuse and neglect case is depicted, which includes a therapist, social worker, teacher, public health nurse, and the abusive mother. Overall improvement in the mother's coping abilities and the parent-child relationship are noted, and professional involvement in the case is removed.

47. National Institute of Mental Health. Focus: Child Abuse and Neglect (Film). 5600 Fishers Lane, Rockville, MD 20852, n.d.

These are multidisciplinary, multiagency training materials which provide information about identification, case management, treatment, and prevention of child abuse. They are intended to help develop an awareness of feelings and attitudes about child abuse, to facilitate an understanding of the necessary components of

(National Institute of Mental Health)

a comprehensive service delivery system for abusive families, and to aid in development of successful models for working with child abuse in local communities. Manuals for instruction are included.

48. New Jersey State Division of Youth and Family Services. A Manual of Staff Development and Training in Protective Services for Provider Agencies. Trenton, NJ: New Jersey State Division of Youth and Family Services, 1975. 168 pages.

The training program for protective service workers in New Jersey is outlined. Trainees are introduced to the problem of abuse and neglect and the characteristics of abused children as well as abusive parents. The role of the Division of Youth and Family Services, its relationship with other agencies, and interagency cooperation are explained. The legal aspects of protective services, which include discussions of the state requirements that affect service worker functions, are explained; recordkeeping, evidence collection, juvenile rights, and court disposition processes are covered. The final chapters in the curriculum concentrate on treatment approaches, typical and atypical child development and supportive-preventive approaches. Extensive use is made of supplemental reading materials drawn from the literature and numerous audiovisual materials.

49. Parents' Magazine Films. Child Abuse and Neglect (Filmstrip). Communications Park Box 3000, Mount Kisco, NY 10549: Guidance Associates, 1975.

This material is for use with parent groups and the general public. This set of five color filmstrips and three cassettes (or one record) distinguishes between discipline and abuse. It points out the use of techniques for prevention and treatment.

50. Paulist Productions. War of the Eggs (Motion Picture). P.O. Box 1057, Pacific Palisades, CA 90272, 1971. 27 minutes.

The child battering syndrome is dramatized by Elizabeth Ashley and Bill Bixby in this motion picture. It focuses on the husband-wife relationship and how it affects the battered child.

51. Schmitt, Barton, ed. The Child Protection Team Handbook. New York, NY: Garland Publishing Co., 1978. 415 pages,

This is a handbook developed for hospital and community based child protection teams. It covers roles of team members, case management procedures, management techniques and policies. The appendices include sample

(Schmitt, Barton)

policies and procedures for managing child abuse.

52. Texas Department of Human Resources. Children in Danger (Slides and cassette tape). Media Services, P.O. Box 2960, Austin, TX 78769, 1974. 11 minutes.

This slide and tape show presents detailed physical indicators of child abuse and neglect. Procedures for reporting suspected cases are given.

53. Texas Department of Human Resources. Sexual Abuse of Children (Videocassette). Media Services, P.O. Box 2960, Austin, TX 78769, 1976. 30 minutes.

This videocassette shows a panel discussion consisting of a child psychiatrist, an attorney, a social worker, and a pediatrician. Part I explains professional viewpoints on sexual abuse of children, violent and non-violent. Part II explores decisions in casework and appropriate actions to take in a suspected child abuse case. Part III discusses case management.

54. Texas Department of Human Resources. This People Business: Child Protective Services; What is Child Abuse? (Videocassette). Media Services, P.O. Box 2960, Austin, TX 78769, 1976. 29 minutes.

Child Protective Services includes an interview with a child welfare worker. The ongoing family unit is discussed, as well as caseloads and termination of parental rights. There are discussions on what a child protective services worker is and what the worker does. It also explains how caseworkers handle their own anger when working with parents who continually abuse their children. What is Child Abuse? is an interview/discussion between a director of family and children's services, a social services director and a physician in an emergency room. Group members explain the first contacts they had with child abuse. The group defines child abuse and neglect and explores the questions of why we have child abuse. Some Texas and nationwide statistics of child abuse are presented.

55. Urzi, Mary (Revised by Margaret Radike). Cooperative Approaches to Child Protection: A Community Guide. St. Paul, MN: Minnesota State Child Abuse and Neglect Division of Social Services, 1980. 137 pages.

This manual provides theoretical and practical guidelines for communities interested in developing a multidisciplinary, community-based approach to child abuse and neglect. Program components, composition and organization of teams are discussed. Other sections

(Urzi, Mary)

deal with setting service/program needs and priorities and barriers to program implementation.

56. Washington University. Stressful Situations (Videotape). Washington University, The George Warren Brown School of Social Work, St. Louis, MO 63130, 1976. 20 minutes.

The kinds of potentially stress-causing reactions a child welfare worker is likely to face when removing children from home and when making a return visit to that home are depicted. The film is recommended for child welfare workers and is most beneficial when a follow-up discussion on the most appropriate response for each situation is included in the program.

57. WQED, Pittsburgh, PA. Broken Homes, Broken Bones (Film). 1309 Cathedral of Learning, Pittsburgh, PA 15260: National Center for Juvenile Justice, 1974. 90 minutes.

Part I of this film depicts the proceedings of a multidisciplinary seminar. The history of child abuse is discussed, as well as the psychodynamics of abusive parents, legal aspects of child abuse and the state of the art with respect to research in the field. Part 2 is a dramatized case of suspected abuse which begins with tentative identification in a hospital and ends with disposition at a juvenile hearing. The investigatory process at the hospital and the court hearing underscore the difficulties surrounding suspected child abuse and appropriate action for such cases.

2

LAW AND COURT

58. Alderman, Marlene. Representation for the Abused and Neglected Child: The Guardian Ad Litem and Legal Counsel. Washington, DC: Administration for Children, Youth and Families, DHHS, 1980. 22 pages.

This brief publication discusses the need for legal representation for children in court. An overview of state legislation is included, along with a list of resource materials and bibliography.

59. American Indian Law Center. Training and Technical Assistance to Develop, Revise and Supplement Indian Tribal Code and Court Procedures on Child Abuse and Neglect (Manual). Albuquerque, NM: University of New Mexico Law School, n.d.

This manual was developed as a supplement about child abuse and neglect procedures and court proceedings for use under the Indian Tribal Code.

60. Baker, Emily, and Dees, Jesse. "How to Prepare Courtroom Presentations." Public Welfare 36 (1978): 30-35.

This article traces the development of the U.S. Juvenile Court system. It describes the responsibilities of social workers who represent child protective agencies in court. It also presents a format for social workers to use in preparation of court reports.

61. Bell, Cynthia. "Legal Consultation for Child Welfare Workers." Public Welfare 33 (1975): 33-40.

The author, a social worker, explains the role of legal consultation in securing protection and permanence for children. A model for legal consultation which was developed in Illinois is described and assessed.

62. Bell, Cynthia and Mlyniec, Wallace. "Preparing for a Neglect Proceeding: A Guide for the Social Worker." Public Welfare 32 (1974): 26-37.

This article provides background information about the Juvenile Court, reviews problems social workers frequently have in court, and explains how agency records can be maintained to be legally usable. It also addresses the issue of hearsay and the use of pretrial conferences.

63. Bernstein, Barton E. "The Social Worker as a Courtroom Witness." Social Casework 56 (1975): 521-525.

This article, written by an attorney, discusses the role of the social worker in court. It is appropriate for direct service child welfare staff, as well as social workers who are called as experts in any types of cases. Although Texas statutes are used for illustrations, most of the material is applicable to other jurisdictions. Preparation for court and actual courtroom behavior is included.

64. Bernstein, Barton E. "The Social Worker as an Expert Witness." Social Casework 58 (1977): 412-417.

This article provides an overview of the role, qualifications, preparation and contributions in court of the expert social work witness. The author is a Texas attorney, and he uses some examples of Texas cases and state law. The information he provides is applicable in most jurisdictions, however. This is a good training reading for child welfare staff who will serve as expert witnesses or select others to testify in court cases.

65. Bernstein, Barton E.; Claman, Lawrence; Harris, Janice C.; and Samson, Judith. "The Child Witness: A Model for Evaluation and Trial Preparation." Child Welfare 61 (1982): 95-104.

This article presents a model for assessing and preparing the child witness. A team which includes legal and mental health staff can use the model to determine the desirability of a particular child testifying in court. All kinds of legal cases are considered.

66. Carrieri, Joseph R. The Foster Child: From Abandonment to Adoption 1980: A Course Handbook. 810 Seventh Avenue, New York, NY 10010: Practising Law Institute, 1980. 395 pages.

Freeing the child for adoption, adoption proceedings and the rights of the child and the natural and foster parents are among the topics examined in this course

(Carrieri, Joseph R.)

handbook, which has been substantially expanded and revised to reflect the current New York law. It was prepared to supplement lectures given in May 1980.

67. Downs, Susan, and Taylor, Catherine. Child Welfare Training: Permanent Planning in Foster Care: Resource for Training. P.O. Box 751, Portland, OR 97207: Regional Research Institute for Human Services, 1980.

Included are: case summaries, articles and excerpts, exercises and a glossary. Emphasis is on the termination of parental rights cases and court preparation and testimony.

68. George Warren Brown School of Social Work, Washington University. Referral Process II: Juvenile Court and Family Services (Videotape). St. Louis, MO 63130, 1976. 15 minutes.

In this black and white videotape, a worker from Juvenile Court and one from Family Services discuss case coordination and their responsibilities in the referral process.

69. Goldstein, Joseph; Freud, Anna; and Solnit, Albert J. Before the Best Interests of the Child. New York: Free Press, 1979. 288 pages.

The authors draw upon legal doctrine, psychoanalytic knowledge, and common sense to examine when and on what grounds the state should intervene in the child's relationship with the family. This challenging book covers such proceedings as neglect, abandonment, abuse, delinquency, foster care, separation, divorce and other family disruption situations.

70. Goldstein, Joseph; Freud, Anna; and Solnit, Albert J. Beyond the Best Interests of the Child. 2nd Edition. New York: Free Press, 1979. 176 pages.

This controversial book has had an enormous impact on the child welfare field and the juvenile court system. Directed at decision making in placement and custody cases, the book stresses the limits of the law in making long-range predictions. The authors argue for placement based on an alternative "least detrimental" to the child rather than his or her "best interests." In this new edition, the authors refine their criticisms of child placement laws and respond to critics of their own child-centered approach. The new epilogue focuses on the issues of visitation and joint custody, adding a new perspective to these problems.

71. Landau, Hortense and others. Child Protection: The Role of the Courts (Manual). Washington, DC: U.S. Government Printing Office, Department 76, 1980. 80 pages.

This manual provides an introduction to the court system, case preparation, use of witnesses, and court ordered treatment. It contains a special section concerning the requirements of the Indial Child Welfare Act.

72. Missouri University, Columbia Academic Support Center. Criminal Court Procedures (Videocassette). 505 East Stewart Road, Columbia, MO 65201, 1975. 31 minutes.

Criminal court procedures in child abuse and neglect cases are outlined, and definitions and laws are provided for first and second degree murder, manslaughter, justifiable homicide, and assault. Provisions pertaining to "in loco parentis" status are cited. The roles of those involved in criminal proceedings (the law enforcement officer, the prosecuting attorney, and the judiciary) are reviewed. Reference is made to the case of a mother imprisoned for child abuse, and the resulting guilt and family problems. The need for treatment rather than punishment for abusive parents is stressed.

73. Missouri University, Columbia Academic Support Center. Juvenile Court Procedures (Videocassette). 505 East Stewart Road, Columbia, MO 65201, 1975. 29 minutes.

Sections of the Missouri juvenile code are cited, and juvenile court procedures are explained. The responsibility of the family services worker to make reports to the juvenile court is noted, stressing the need for providing factual information and avoiding opinions, jargon, and vague terminology. The two phases of the juvenile court hearing, the adjudicatory phase and the dispositional phase, are reviewed. The process of appealing a case is also discussed. The tape has limited applicability to other jurisdictions.

74. Missouri University, Columbia Academic Support Center. Presenting the Case (Videocassette or Film). 505 East Stewart Road, Columbia, MO 65201, 1975. 32 minutes.

The testimony of the family services worker is reviewed in a simulated court hearing. A case history is presented and the role of the worker is defined. Explanations and evaluations of the questions asked and the testimony given during the hearing are provided by the narrator. Emphasis is placed on the importance of the social worker remaining calm, answering concisely, being honest and identifying his role and qualifications.

75. Mooney, William B. The Social Worker and Doctor in Court (Videotape). Box 3623, University Station, Laramie, WY 82070: University of Wyoming Department of Social Work, n.d. 240 minutes.

This tape was produced at the University of Iowa, but is now available from the author at the above address. It shows simulated testimony and cross-examination in a child abuse and neglect case. The pediatrician, social worker and judge who appear in the simulation are professionals in their fields. The medical witness is portrayed giving strong evidence about the case. The social worker is shown twice, first as a poorly prepared witness and then as an excellent one. The social worker's testimony is shown to be the determining factor in the outcome of the court case.

76. Mussell, Frank. "The Social Worker as a Courtroom Witness: Cruel and Unusual Punishment." Connection (June 1977).

This article provides a discussion of how the social worker can better prepare to give testimony in court. Reprints can be obtained from Regional Research Institute for Human Services, P. O. Box 751, Portland, OR 97207.

77. National Association of Attorneys General. Legal Issues in Foster Care. Committee on the Office of Attorney General, 3901 Barrett Drive, Raleigh, NC 27609, 1976. 59 pages.

This detailed manual cites important court decisions and typical and atypical state laws and regulations concerning: termination of parental rights, rights of foster parents, subsidized adoptions, right to counsel and model acts. It would provide good background for court workers, administrators, and staff or consulting attorneys.

78. National Center for the Prevention and Treatment of Child Abuse and Neglect. A Self-Instructional Audio-Visual Program for Professionals: The Role of the Juvenile Court Judge (Videotape). University of Colorado Medical Center, Denver, CO 80220, 1976. 30 minutes.

Excerpts from an interview with Judge James Delaney of Colorado are presented. The focus is on his views about child abuse and neglect and how courts can intervene positively with abusive families.

79. National Center on Child Abuse and Neglect. We Can Help: A Curriculum on the Identification, Reporting, Referral, and Case Management of Child Abuse and Neglect (NCCAN Curriculum - Multi-Media). P.O. Box 1182, Washington, DC 20013, 1975.

Three units from this training package pertain to law and the courts. The Role of the Courts (Unit 11), provides a film and manual which can be presented in 2 hours. It gives an overview of the functions and purposes of criminal and juvenile courts in child abuse and neglect cases. Procedures for handling a case of suspected abuse or neglect are outlined. Presenting the Case (Unit 13), a 32 minute film, shows a social worker testifying in a juvenile court child abuse hearing. The Medical Witness (Unit 14), a 35 minute film, dramatizes a physician as a witness in a juvenile court child abuse case.

80. National Institute of Mental Health, Department of Health and Human Services. Doctor in Court (Film). 5600 Fishers Lane, Rockville, MD 20852, 1976. 31 minutes.

The film dramatizes a pre-trial briefing and a courtroom trial. It is designed to improve testimony by physicians in child abuse and neglect proceedings. The film notes precautions to be taken during cross-examination. This advice is intended to prepare the physician to present unequivocal statements about his diagnosis.

81. Region VI Resource Center on Child Abuse and Neglect. Dallas-Fort Worth Mental Health Association Conference on Child Abuse and Neglect: Judge James Delaney (Videotape). University of Texas School of Social Work, 2609 University Avenue, Austin, TX 78712, 1976. 30 minutes.

Judge Delaney discusses the constructive use of the law in the prevention and treatment of child abuse. He outlines the rights and responsibilities of the child, the parents, and the community, and explains how the legal component of a multidisciplinary team affects child abuse and neglect efforts.

82. Region VI Resource Center on Child Abuse and Neglect. The Psychiatric Expert in the Case of an Emotionally Maltreated Child (Videocassette). University of Texas School of Social Work, 2609 University Avenue, Austin, TX 78712, 1978. 45 minutes.

This is a dramatization of the courtroom experience of a psychiatrist testifying in an emotional abuse case. It presents a realistic view of direct and cross-examination, an aid in preparing psychiatrists and other professionals for the potential pressure and problems of appearing as a witness in legal proceedings.

83. Region VI Resource Center on Child Abuse and Neglect. The Social Worker as a Witness (Videotape or videocassette). University of Texas School of Social Work, 2609 University Avenue, Austin, TX 78712, 1976. 55 minutes.

This dramatization of the courtroom experience of a child welfare worker presents a realistic view of direct and cross-examination. It is intended as an aid in preparing a case worker for the potential pressures and problems of appearing as a witness in legal proceedings. A manual is also available.

84. Rose, Carol M. Some Emerging Issues in Legal Liability of Children's Agencies. New York: Child Welfare League of America, Inc., 1978. 68 pages.

In the past few years, judicial decisions have had measurable impact on the operation of child welfare agencies. Carol M. Rose explores these decisions and their implications for such explosive issues as the rights of children, invasion of privacy, termination of parental rights, the rights of foster and adopted parents, and issues of record keeping and disclosure. An appendix lists the landmark cases and statutes that have played major roles in current child welfare litigation.

85. Texas Department of Human Resources. Child Advocacy Resources Expansion Project (Film). P.O. Box 2960, Austin, TX 78769: Media Services Division, 1976. 60 minutes.

This training film presents a mock civil court trial of parents accused of abusing a child. The film illustrates the presentation of the evidence and focuses on the roles of the judge and attorneys.

86. University of Wisconsin Center for Social Service. Legal Training for Child Welfare Workers (Videocassettes and Manuals). University of Wisconsin Extension, 610 Langdon Street, Madison, WI 53706, 1975.

This is a comprehensive training program designed to provide social workers, supervisors and agency directors in Wisconsin with information and skills to enhance their effectiveness in judicial and legislative matters involving their client populations. Videocassette programs of approximately one hour each focus on: legal bibliography due process in delinquency proceedings; legal issues in protective services; termination of parental rights; courtroom procedures and strategies; grantsmanship and funding; innovative services; and proposed revisions of the children's code. The training manual contains supportive training formats and a bibliography for each program. The series may be presented as a complete unit, or parts may be used separately to meet agency and staff needs.

87. Wald, Michael S. "State Intervention on Behalf of 'Neglected' Children: Standards for Removal of Children from their Homes, Monitoring the Status of Children in Foster Care, and Termination of Parents' Rights." Stanford Law Review 28 (1976): 623-702.

This well-known article gives an overview of the shortcomings of the foster care system and proposes extensive reform of the laws which govern entry into and exit from foster care.

88. Welfare Research, Inc. Freeing Children for Adoption A State of the Art Report. 112 State Street, Albany, NY 12207, 1978. 90 pages.

This report describes existing legal training programs for social workers in New York State and presents issues to be addressed in developing a legal training program for statewide use. It will be interesting to those developing training in other states.

3

SUBSTITUTE CARE

89. Baker, Cynthia C., and Hegar, Rebecca L., eds. Methods of Integrating Child Welfare Content in Undergraduate Programs. Proceedings from Workshops for Undergraduate Program Faculty. New Orleans, LA 70118: Region VI Child Welfare Training Center, Tulane University School of Social Work, 1981. 74 pages.

This compendium of course materials includes a keynote presentation by Betty Baer, "Emphasis at the BSW Level--The Case of Child Welfare." Other presentations concern the undergraduate child welfare sequence, "The Course in Child Welfare," and the field instruction component. A model detailed course plan and a number of course syllabi are included.

90. Baker, Cynthia C., and Hegar, Rebecca L., eds. The Search for Permanency: Home Based Services to Families and Children. Proceedings from Workshops for Graduate Program Faculty. November, 1980. New Orleans, LA 70118: Region VI Child Welfare Training Center, Tulane University School of Social Work, 1981. 182 pages.

This collection of training materials concerns planning for children in foster care to return to their own homes, as well as home-based services which prevent removal and placement. A keynote presentation by Marvin Bryce is entitled "Home-Based Family-Centered Services." Other presentations focus on teaching permanency planning and family alliances, and on parent education as a tool in permanency planning. Several course syllabi which were shared in an information exchange are included. A number of excellent bibliographies are also reproduced here.

91. Cassette Communications, Inc. Adoption: A Guide for Parents and Professionals (Audiocassette). 175 Fifth Avenue, New York, NY 10010, n.d.

Two adoption services personnel discuss guidelines for deciding on adoption, criteria for choosing an agency, and factors which should be considered after adoption. Placement philosophies are presented, and the differences between foster care and adoption are explained, stressing the differences in the legal rights of both parents and children.

92. Cautler, Patricia Woodward. New Foster Parents: The First Experience. New York: Human Sciences Press, 1980.

This book traces the experiences of 107 new foster families from their initial interview with the social agency when first applying for foster care, through their first placement of a school-age child for a maximum of eighteen months. The author examines the relationship of the foster parents' feelings about their new role with various aspects of the placement, including the kind of child placed, the involvement of the child's natural family, the social worker's input, and the foster parents' relative success in meeting the needs of the child. The findings will be of practical value to social workers to help them identify the more promising foster parents at the time of their interview.

93. Chestang, Leon. "The Dilemma of Biracial Adoption." Social Work 17 (1972): 100-105.

This short article lists and discusses the pros and cons of biracial adoption. It develops the idea that there are no clear answers to the questions surrounding interracial adoptions.

94. Child Welfare League of America. Don't Condemn Me Till You Know Me (Film). 67 Irving Place, New York, NY 10003, n.d. 24 minutes.

This film depicts five foster parents discussing their feelings about relationships with their children, the social workers and foster parents.

95. Child Welfare League of America. Foster Parenting a Retarded Child (Multimedia). 67 Irving Place, New York, NY 10003, n.d.

Foster parents discuss the capabilities and individuality of retarded foster children and are helped to develop realistic expectations. Sessions are designed to help foster parents analyze their feelings, needs, responsibilities, as well as sharpen skills. The package includes manuals, films and audiocassettes.

96. Child Welfare League of America. Foster Parenting an Adolescent (Multimedia). 67 Irving Place, New York, NY 10003, 1977.

Designed as a series of seven 2-hour sessions, foster parents discuss the kinds of situations apt to occur and the special aspects of parenting a foster adolescent This course will enhance understanding of oneself, increase sensitivity about adolescents and develop effective ways of responding to teen-age foster children Topics include: "The Things Kids Do: Adolescent Behavior," "What's Going On: Adolescent Development," "Talking with Teens: Listening and Responding," "Living with Teens: Ways of Getting Along," "On Their Own: Adolescent Life Tasks," "Giving and Getting: Relationships," and "Getting it Together: Personal Identity." (The package includes 2 films, 2 audio tapes, readings and materials for trainers.)

97. Child Welfare League of America. Identifying Family Issues in the Adoption of Children with Developmental Disabilities: Using the Genogram (Videocassette). 67 Irving Place, New York, NY 10003, n.d. 110 minutes (3 parts).

Part 1 presents a model for collecting data for the genogram and illustrates how the data is then used to begin assessing the dynamics of the family being interviewed. Part 2 shows an interview with a family interested in adopting a child with a handicapping condition; the social worker is shown with the family, pursuing the issues that surfaced in the development of the genogram. Part 3 depicts a supervisory conference in which the interviewer and the supervisor identify issues for this family that are most relevant to the adoption of a handicapped child. A training manual is included.

98. Child Welfare League of America. Introduction to Foster Parenting (Multimedia). 67 Irving Place, New York, NY 10003: Foster Parent Curriculum Project, 1976.

This series of six 2-hour sessions for new and prospective foster parents is designed to promote a greater awareness of the basic issues involved in fostering. It is designed specifically to be taught by agency personnel. Course topics include: "What is Foster Parenting," "The Foster Child in our Home," "Our Foster Child's Natural Parents," "Working with the Agency," and "You, the Agency and Community Placement." The course materials include a leader's guide, workbooks and readings, 3 films, audio tapes and visual aids.

99. Child Welfare League of America. Somebody Talk to Me (Film). 67 Irving Place, New York, NY 10003, n.d. 15 minutes.

This film presents the thoughts and feelings of five foster children. It includes their reactions to separation, feelings about their foster and biological families, and the children's understanding of the reasons for foster care placement. The film is useful for staff development, foster parent and natural parent groups.

100. Child Welfare League of America. The Worker: Social Work in Foster Family--An Overview with Emphasis on the Role of the Social Worker (Film). 67 Irving Place, New York, NY 10003, n.d. 11 minutes.

This film follows a social worker through a day of foster care related activities: appointments, conferences and conversations about the foster children in his caseload.

101. Child Welfare League of America. With a Little Help from our Friends: A Collection of Readings for Foster Parenting an Adolescent. New York. Child Welfare League of America, 1977. 82 pages.

This book, part of the CWLA training package about adolescent foster care, can also be used separately in foster parent or worker training. Readings are brief, simple and practice oriented. Several represent the adolescent's viewpoint.

102. Children's Home Society of Cincinnati. Albert Lee (Videotape). 5051 Duck Creek Road, Cincinnati, OH 45227, 1976. 30 minutes.

This videotape portrays a 19-year-old black adoptee who is seeking background information about himself and is searching for his bio-mother. It is excellent for staff development and adoptive parent education.

103. Children's Home Society of Cincinnati. Bill (Videotape). 5051 Duck Creek Road, Cincinnati, OH 45227, 1976. 130 minutes.

A 13-year-old youngster is adopted by a childless couple. They talk about their adjustmements to family life. This is an excellent film for potential adoptive parents of older children.

104. Children's Home Society of Cincinnati. Debbie (Videotape). 5051 Duck Creek Road, Cincinnati, OH 45227, 1976. 15 minutes.

A 21 year-old adoptee returns to the agency seeking information about her background. Debbie raises the question, "Who am I?" and describes her feelings of being rejected by her bio-mother. The information that is given to her relieves her feelings of rejection. This film is good for adoptive parent education and staff training.

105. Children's Home Society of Cincinnati. Francie (Videotape). 5051 Duck Creek Road, Cincinnati, OH 45227, n.d. 20 minutes.

In a post-placement interview, a 19 year-old discusses her 26 foster home placements, her feeling and perceptions about herself and the help she received from the staff at the center.

106. Children's Home Society of Cincinnati. Hilary (Videotape). 5051 Duck Creek Road, Cincinnati, OH 45227, 1976. 30 minutes.

The videotape focuses on unmarried parents. The tape presents Hilary, a 20 year-old woman, who, as an unmarried teenager, surrendered a child for adoption. She describes her life and expresses her hopes that some day her child will search for her.

107. Children's Home Society of Cincinnati. Interpretive Tapes (Videotape). 5051 Duck Creek Road, Cincinnati, OH 45227, 1976. 60 minutes.

This tape shows six unmarried mothers discussing their views about surrendering their children for adoption. The mothers also discuss their views about adoptee searches for identity. It is useful for staff training and parent groups.

108. Children's Home Society of Cincinnati. John (Videotape). 5051 Duck Creek Road, Cincinnati, OH 45227, 1976. 60 minutes.

An 18 year-old describes his feelings and those of his adoptive and biological mothers. The role of the social worker as an intermediary is also discussed in this film. It is useful for board and staff training. The film should be viewed along with John's Adoptive Mother.

109. Children's Home Society of Cincinnati. John's Adoptive Mother (Videotape). 5051 Duck Creek Road, Cincinnati, OH 45227, n.d. 33 minutes.

This videotape describes an adoptive mother's feeling about John's search for his biological parents. It is an excellent tape for adoptive parent discussion groups.

110. Children's Home Society of Cincinnati. Kim (Videotape). 5051 Duck Creek Road, Cincinnati, OH 45227, n.d. 30 minutes.

This tape depicts a 7 year-old black handicapped girl with an audio memory defect. She has had two adoption failures. She is shown playing with her social worker, who describes Kim's problems. This is a good illustration of how to use video to recruit families for special needs children. It is also good for staff development.

111. Children's Home Society of Cincinnati. Marlene, Parts 1 and 2 (Videotape). 5051 Duck Creek Road, Cincinnati, OH 45227, n.d. Part 1, 10 minutes; Part 2, 60 minutes.

Part 1 introduces a 20 year-old adoptee who discusses her rejection by her adoptive parents and her search for her biological mother. She was adopted at infancy. It is excellent for educating prospective adoptive parents and also good for general staff discussion on the issues of search. Part 2 described Marlene's anxieties and experience after reunion with her biological mother four months later.

112. Children's Home Society of Cincinnati. Mr. and Mrs. Levy (Videotape). 5051 Duck Creek Road, Cincinnati, OH 45227, 1976. 60 minutes.

This tape focuses on some of the dynamics of the adjustment phase of adoption placement. A couple discuss the changes in family life that were necessary with the addition of an older child to the family. It is useful for staff training and adoptive parent groups.

113. Children's Home Society of Cincinnati. Teen-Age Father (Film). 5051 Duck Creek Road, Cincinnati, OH 45227, n.d. 30 minutes.

This film portrays the teenage father's feelings about his girlfriend's pregnancy. Many facets of this dilemma are touched on in a sensitive and realistic presentation. It is very useful for teenage discussion groups and staff development.

114. Children's Home Society of Cincinnati. Tony--Unmarried Father (Videotape). 5051 Duck Creek Road, Cincinnati, OH 45227, n.d. 25 minutes.

A young man who participated in the surrender of his daughter for adoption describes this participation and his feelings of pain because of the surrender. He also describes the help he received from the social worker. This view of the unmarried father's thoughts and feelings is useful for adoptive parents and unmarried parent groups.

115. Children's Home Society of Cincinnati. "Why" of Adoptees' Search for Identity (Videotape). 5051 Duck Creek Road, Cincinnati, OH 45227, n.d. 60 minutes.

This videotape presents excerpts of an interview with adoptees who discuss their feelings and thoughts about why they decided to search for their birth parents. It is a useful film for staff discussion, and board and adoptive parent education.

116. Churchill, Sallie R.; Carlson, Bonnie; and Nybell, Lynn, eds. No Child is Unadoptable: A Reader on Adoption of Children with Special Needs. Beverly Hills: Sage Publications, 1979. 172 pages.

The problems and solutions of a service agency attempting to find a permanent home for the child with atypical needs, for the child with minority heritage, or for the older child, are the subject matter of this volume. The contributors examine such topics as the evaluation of potential adoptive families and children, single parent adoption, the adoption of children with special medical problems, transracial adoption, and disruption of the foster care/adoptive family cycle.

117. Citizen's Committee for Children of New York, Inc. The Parents' Rights Unit: Responding to Grievances of Parents with Children in Foster Care. 105 East 22nd Street, New York, NY 10010, 1977. 23 pages.

This manual is an evaluation of the first months of operation of the Parents' Rights Unit of New York City's Department of Special Services for Children. While this material is applicable largely to New York, it is one of few resources available concerning the rights of parents. The primary audience for the report includes administrators, attorneys, and evaluators of similar programs. The results of a national survey on the handling of parental complaints are reported briefly.

118. Day, Dawn. The Adoption of Black Children: Counter-Acting Institutional Discrimination. Lexington, PA: Lexington Books, 1979. 156 pages.

This book centers on the needs of black children for adoption homes, the discrimination which often blocks adoptive placement of blacks, and the organization of the adoptive system. The author writes in some detail about how adoption opportunities for black children can be improved. Adoption into both black and non-black homes is considered.

119. Downs, Susan. Foster Care Reform in the '70's: Final Report of the Permanency Planning Dissemination Project. P.O. Box 751, Portland, OR 97207: Regional Research Institute for Human Services, 1980. 300 pages.

This manual reviews the work done by the Dissemination Project, summarizes the permanency planning activities of each state, and makes recommendations for future development of permanency planning efforts.

120. Downs, Susan, and Taylor, Catherine. Permanent Planning in Foster Care: Resources for Training. P.O. Box 751, Portland, OR 97207: Regional Research Institute for Human Services, 1978. 264 pages.

This book is a compilation of training resources to be used with students and caseworkers to teach permanent planning for children in foster care. The two major sections of the book concern direct services and legal skills. Sample cases, readings, and exercises are included.

121. Dreyer, Linda. Permanent Planning in Foster Care: A Guide for Program Planners. P.O. Box 751, Portland, OR 97207: Regional Research Institute for Human Services, 1978. 104 pages.

This is a manual for administrators involved in building new programs to promote permanency planning.

122. Emlen, Arthur, and others. Overcoming Barriers to Planning for Children in Foster Care. P.O. Box 751, Portland, OR 97207: Regional Research Institute for Human Services, 1977. 121 pages.

This is the second in the series of reports on the Oregon demonstration project which was officially called "Freeing Children for Permanent Placement." This handbook gives background on the project, describes how barriers were overcome, provides a case history, and explains the role of legal representation for the child.

123. EPD Consortium C. The Realities of Adolescent Care: Staff Training (Slide-tape show and Manual). Austin, TX 78701: Texas Department of Human Resources, Media Services, 1978.

The significant content areas include: adolescents in foster care, group care and institutional care; contracting to maintain placements; adolescent growth and development; recruitment, selection, supervision and evaluation of foster parents; and the use of volunteers.

124. Felker, Evelyn H. Foster Parenting Young Children. New York, NY: Child Welfare League of America, 1979. 85 pages.

Out of her own experiences as a foster mother, the author offers a perceptive, compassionate guide to caring for young foster children. Unique in child welfare literature, her book covers all aspects of being a foster parent, the caseworker and the agency, and the foster parent association, Mrs. Felker shows how to use the whole experience for personal growth and satisfaction.

125. Films, Incorporated. The Kreimeik and Bosworth Families (Videocassette or Film). 1144 Wilmette Avenue, Wilmette, IL 60091, n.d. 7 minutes.

Only a few years ago, the idea of unmarried people adopting children was unheard of. The Kreimeik and Bosworth families of Denver are indicative of changing times. Ms. Kreimeik had a pleasant life-style and no regrets about not having married, but she yearned for children. Her two daughters, adopted in infancy, have given her fulfillment. Bruce Bosworth's sex was against him and it was five years before his two older boys, children from the Saigon baby lift, were placed with him. His youngest, eight-year-old Paul, is handicapped.

126. Group Child Care Consultant Service. The Basic Course for Residential Child Care Workers (Manual). School of Social Work, University of North Carolina, Chapel Hill, NC 27514, 1977.

This program was developed for residential child care workers in institutional organizations or group homes serving the following types of children: dependent/neglected, juvenile delinquent, emotionally disturbed, physically handicapped, and mentally retarded. Consisting of seven modules dealing with specific aspects of residential care, the program can be used as a self-instruction course. Each module has a student manual, written as programmed instruction, and instructor's manual that offers a variety of teaching strategies.

127. Grow, Lucille, J., and Shapiro, Deborah. Transracial Adoption Today. New York: Child Welfare League of America, 1976. 91 pages.

This book reports on research concerning attitudes toward transracial adoption in four regions of the U.S.: Massachusetts, California, Minnesota, and Washington State. Only placements of black children in white families were studied. Both agency staff and adoptive families were interviewed concerning racial attitudes.

128. Guerney, Louise F. Foster Parent Training: A Manual for Parents. P.O. Box 319, State College, PA 16801: Ideals, 1977.

This manual, which was designed to be used by foster parents in conjunction with a training program, systematically teaches communication and behavior management skills. It explains the skills, provides a rationale, and offers examples, practice exercises and homework.

129. Guerney, Louise F. Foster Parent Training: A Manual for Trainers. P.O. Box 319, State College, PA 16801: Ideals, 1977.

This manual is intended for trainers of foster parents. It includes parenting skills also found in companion manuals for parents, as well as group leadership skills. Objectives, lecture outline, general suggestions, and practice exercises are included for each session.

130. Guerney, Louise F. Foster Parent Training: Adolescent Supplement. P.O. Box 319, State College, PA 16801: n.d.

This manual was specifically designed to help foster parents use communication and behavior management skills with adolescents.

131. Harris, Grace E. Training Public Welfare Staff in the Use of the Service Contract in Preventing and Reducing Foster Care. Hampton, VA 23669: Service Contract Project, Hampton Department of Social Services, 1320 LaSalle Avenue, 1978. 34 pages.

This report describes the training component of a federally funded project designed to demonstrate the use of service contracting. It presents the theory and training methodology used and explores situations in which contracting may be most appropriate.

132. Hartman, Ann. Finding Families: An Ecological Approach to Family Assessment in Adoption. Beverly Hills: Sage Publications, 1979. 108 pages.

This text is designed to aid social workers in adoption practice, particularly in the complex family assessment process that is so central to effective child placement. In the guide, a model of a family assessment is presented in a step-by-step fashion as a shared process occurring between adoptive applicants and adoption workers. Growing out of an ecological systems perspective that views individuals and their families as open systems deeply immersed in their environments, the assessment model includes specific tools that translate the ecological perspective into practice.

133. Harvest A-V, Inc. Bridge to Adoption (Film). 309 Fifth Avenue, New York, NY 10016, 1967. 27 minutes.

The film illustrates the steps in the adoption process through three case situations. Adoption workers conduct interviews with prospective adoptors in the initial, application and evaluative phases.

134. Hegar, Rebecca L., ed. Parent Education of Groups with Mexican-American Child Welfare Clients. New Orleans, LA 70118: Region VI Child Welfare Training Center, Tulane University School of Social Work, 1982. 91 pages.

This volume of four papers presents an overview of parent education approaches, introduces the Cognitive/Small Group Model which was developed at Tulane University, and concludes with material about adapting that model to meet the needs of Mexican-American parents. A copy of a "Parents' Handbook" developed for a demonstration parent education group in Texas is included.

135. Heinritz, G., and Frey, L. Foster Care: How to Develop An Educational Program for Staff of Foster Parents (Manual). Boston University School of Social Work, Division of Continuing Education, 264 Bay State Road, Boston, MA 02215, n.d.

Resources for the development of individually-tailored training programs for foster care workers and foster parents are presented. The focus is on the content (knowledge, attitude and skills) needed for good practice in foster family care, and a methodology for assessing learner needs, and planning and implementing an educational program.

136. Horejsi, Charles R. Foster Family Care: A Handbook for Social Workers, Allied Professionals and Concerned Citizens. Springfield, IL: Charles C. Thomas, 1979. 357 pages.

In a question and answer format, this text covers many commonly asked questions about foster care. It is appropriate for new child welfare staff or undergraduates or graduate social worker students. One chapter addresses issues in foster care for American Indian children.

137. Illinois Department of Children and Family Services. Adoption Handbook (Manual). 2020 West Roosevelt Road, Chicago, IL 60608, 1976.

This manual covers the adoption process, from the evaluation phase through the release of guardianship after the adoption is final. In its present form it is applicable primarily to Illinois.

138. Image Associates. The Children's Group--Preparing for Adoption (Film). P.O. Box 40106, Santa Barbara, CA 93103, n.d. 17 minutes.

This film depicts a group of foster children discussing their feelings about foster care and adoption. The group is led by two social workers who help the children examine their thoughts and feelings. The film is designed to be used to train social workers with limited experience in working with children's groups. The function of the group is to supplement caseworker's efforts by enabling children to interact with their peers and discuss common experiences. Other appropriate viewers are prospective adoptive parents who are interested in learning about various backgrounds of children awaiting placement.

139. Image Associates. The Parents' Group--Working with the Adoptive Family. P.O. Box 40106, Santa Barbara, CA 93102. 19 minutes.

In this film, a group of adoptive parents discuss the challenges associated with integrating an older child into a family. It is primarily designed as a training film for social workers who have had limited experience in leading post-placement groups. Adoptive families and older children are possible audiences of the film if given appropriate preparation.

140. Image Associates. The Scrapbook Experience--Building A Child's Identity (Film). P.O. Box 40106, Santa Barbara, CA 93103, n.d. 16 minutes.

The process by which a foster child develops a sense of identity by making an autobiographical scrapbook is illustrated. The child is guided by a social worker who encourages him to think about his past and express his feelings. The film is primarily intended for use as a training tool for social workers who help children deal with past life experiences. It may also be useful with foster and adoptive parents in demonstrating the value of preserving mementos and photographs from the child's past. Foster children may also potentially benefit from viewing the film by being stimulated to share their own feelings and experiences.

141. Jones, Martha, and Biesecker, John. Goal Planning in Children and Youth Services. Division of Training and Technical Assistance, Administration for Children, Youth and Families, DHHS, Washington, DC 20201, 1980. 52 pages.

The manual consists of five lessons designed to give the worker experience in writing and developing permanent plans for children. Sessions include exercises, case examples and suggestions for work with difficult clients. These should prepare the worker to write clear, reasonable and measurable goals for himself and for clients.

142. Kadushin, Alfred. Adopting Older Children. New York: Columbia University Press, 1970. 245 pages.

This book reports on a group of parents who accepted a child for adoption when the child was five years of age or older. Presented primarily in the parents' own words are portraits of some of the joys and satisfactions, sorrows and disappointments that resulted from welcoming the older child into the family.

143. Kansas State University. Foster Parent Education Curriculum (Manuals). Department of Family and Child Development, Room 143, Justin Hall, Foster Parent Project, Manhattan, KS 66505, 1976.

This curriculum package for foster parent training comprises a foundation book and seven units including more specific curriculum materials. Two volumes contain the teaching units, a chart of competencies, materials written for the instructor, suggested teaching strategies, discussion guides and resources.

144. Kaplan, Bert L., and Seitz, Martin. The Practical Guide to Foster Family Care. Springfield, IL: Charles C. Thomas, 1980.

This handbook is primarily for foster parents. It discusses the practical aspects of everyday life in the foster family. Relationships with foster children, biological familes, and agency social workers receive detailed treatment. A section about discipline is included, as is one about separation and transitions.

145. Kline, Draza, and Overstreet, Helen-Mary Forbush. Foster Care of Children: Nurture and Treatment. New York: Columbia University Press, 1972. 384 pages.

Written by well-known and highly experienced leaders in foster care, the book spans the placement process from intake to discharge. Case illustrations are use extensively.

146. Kuczkowski, Paul J.; Green, Shia T.; Stewart, Rachel; and Leonard, John W. Permanent Planning in Maryland: A Manual for the Foster Care Worker. 11 South Street, Baltimore, MD 21202: Director of Social Services, Administration, 1978. 60 pages.

This manual is an outcome of the Maryland Foster Care Impact Demonstration Project. It is intended to be a "how to do it and by when" guide for child welfare workers. While it was written for Maryland workers, much of the material is applicable to other states. The format, procedures, and model forms may be useful to other agencies which are developing manuals for their states.

147. Lauffer, Armand, and others. Resources for Child Placement and Other Human Services. Beverly Hills: Sage Publications, 1979. 192 pages.

The orchestration of available resources and the creation of new resources are fundamental to the effective functioning of any human service agency. This guide offers a concrete approach to the development of such resources for children requiring placement such as adoption or foster care, but may be applied in a wide range of social service settings. Examinations of program resources, strategic resources, and people as resources are accompanied by appropriate exercises, simulation games, and checklists for prospecting and developing resources.

148. Little, Arthur D., Inc. Foster Parenting. 1735 1st Street, N.W., Washington, DC 20001, 1978. 74 pages.

This manual is designed to guide foster care workers through the processes of selecting and training

(Little, Arthur D., Inc.)

foster parents. The benefits to the foster child and caseworker of having qualified foster parents are noted.

149. Los Angeles County Department of Adoptions. Children's Group (Film). 67 Irving Place, New York, NY 10003: Child Welfare League of America, 1976. 17 minutes.

This film portrays an actual therapy group of school-aged children who are being prepared for adoption. The film shows how the group encourages each child to express his feelings about foster care and his new adoptive home, including the anxieties and fears surrounding these experiences. It is a good film for training staff and parent groups.

150. Los Angeles County Department of Adoptions. One of the Family (Film). 67 Irving Place, New York, NY 10003: Child Welfare League of America, 1976. 27 minutes.

Designed to help prepare adoptive applicants, the film offers a glimpse into the future for those who decide to take an older child into their home. The film illustrates the mutual adjustments which must take place before a child really becomes one of the family. It is also useful for staff training.

151. Los Angeles County Department of Adoptions. Parents' Group (Film). 67 Irving Place, New York, NY 10003: Child Welfare League of America, 1976. 19 minutes.

This film depicts how an agency works with adoptive families. It affords workers the opportunity to pick up on good supervisory techniques. The group consists of parents who have had older children recently paced with them. The workers deal with the specific adjustment problems each family is having in addition to their ambivalent feelings about parenthood.

152. Maluccio, Anthony N., and Sinanoglu, Paula A. The Challenge of Partnership: Working with Parents of Children in Foster Care. New York: Child Welfare League of America, 1981. 225 pages.

This book of eleven original papers offers background, philosophy, and a spectrum of approaches and programs for incorporating work with parents in the entire placement process. Through its explicit focus on parents, the authors advance recent efforts to raise child placement to a new stage of development and promise. Agencies will find that this volume holds a tool for revitalizing placement casework. It is appropriate for use in the classroom as a definitive text on planning for permanency.

153. Murphy, Gwendolyn. Foster Care of the Developmentally Disabled: A Basic Course for Foster Parents and Foster Care Workers. 264 Bay State Road, Boston, MA 02215: Boston University School of Social Work, Division of Continuing Education, 1975. 154 pages.

This manual has been developed as part of a project called "Certificate Program in Foster Care of the Developmentally Disabled," which was funded by the Massachusetts Developmental Disabilities Council. As reported in the manual, the goals and objectives of the project reflect the Council's priority of developing special living arrangements for the developmentally disabled. The project attempted to accomplish this through the education of those who provide such arrangements. A second goal was to encourage foster parents in the traditional public and private child welfare agencies, through education, to accept disabled individuals into their homes.

154. North American Center on Adoption. Recruitment: Sherri Bunnin (Videotape). 67 Irving Place, New York, NY 10003, 1976. 30 minutes.

This videotape describes the successful efforts of an adoptive parent group to recruit families for children with special needs. Techniques discussed would be useful for an agency staff which is developing a recruitment program.

155. O'Connell, Marie H. Helping the Child to Use Foster Family Care. Child Welfare League of America, 1953. 39 pages.

This training booklet covers the principles and practical aspects of the social worker's role with parents, foster parents and children. Although it is almost 30 years old, this remains one of the most widely used statements of the social work role in child welfare.

156. Phillips, Michael H.; Haring, Barbara L.; and Shyne, Ann W. A Model for Intake Decisions in Child Welfare. New York: Child Welfare League of America, 1972. 100 pages.

Decision making at intake is the first and most influential determinant of what will happen to children and families who come to a child welfare agency. This book offers a field-tested guide to history-taking in a semi-structured interview which can be copied by the purchaser for staff use.

157. Pike, Victor A., and others. Permanent Planning for Children in Foster Care: A Handbook for Social Workers. P.O. Box 751, Portland, OR 98202: Regional Research Institute for Human Services, 1977. 142 pages.

This is one volume of the series of publications resulting from the Oregon Project, "Freeing Children for Permanent Placement." This manual is a practical guide to assist the worker in analyzing available placements and choosing the appropriate one. Major sections deal with the need for permanency planning, assessing barriers in a particular case, structuring treatment programs, choosing alternative permanent plans, freeing children for adoption, and preparing termination cases.

158. Possin, C., Citizens' Coalition for Children. Comprehensive Training Program in Adoption for New York State (Manual). Research Utilization Program Services, State Department of Social Services, 40 North Pearl Street, Albany, NY 12243, 1977.

This document presents a detailed outline for developing a statewide training program for adoption workers. A description is provided of the needs assessment study that was conducted to define the scope and goals of the proposed curriculum. The resulting goals were: to improve adoption services for waiting children; to increase the number of adoptive services; to implement new ideas through involvement of community leaders; to increase cooperation between workers in a region; and to increase involvement of child care workers in innovations and trends. It is useful in other states, as well as in New York.

159. Raynor, Lois. The Adopted Child Comes of Age. London: George Allen & Unwin, 1980. 166 pages.

This book reports a British follow-up study of over 100 adopted children who are now young adults. It addresses the questions of how adoptees feel about their families and themselves. It also looks at the gaps between the expectations of adoptive couples and the achievements of their adopted children. Much of this material can be adapted for training.

160. Regional Research Institute for Human Services. Everybody's Children (Filmstrip). P.O. Box 751, Portland, OR 97207, n.d. 13 minutes.

This filmstrip is aimed at citizens and professionals who may become involved in permanent planning. It points out the problems of unplanned foster care and explains the roles that judges, lawyers, legislators, citizen advocates and social service professionals can play.

161. Regional Research Institute for Human Services. His Name is Today (Filmstrip with Audiocassette). P.O. Box 751, Portland, OR 97207, n.d. 11 minutes.

Aimed at professionals in the field of social work, this program introduces the problem of foster care drift and documents some of the experiences and methods that caseworkers have used to achieve permanent homes for children in foster care.

162. Regional Research Institute for Human Services. Permanent Planning Casework: The Initial Interview (Videocassette). P.O. Box 751, Portland, OR 97207, n.d. 15 minutes.

A dramatized interview of a parent whose child is in foster care is featured. The tape presents the problems a permanent planning caseworker is likely to encounter in working with the parents of children in foster care and suggests strategies for overcoming these problems. It also discusses the parent's understanding of the caseworker's explanation of the necessity for permanent planning, the option of voluntary relinquinshment, and other options based on the child's needs for a permanent home.

163. Robertson, James, and Robertson, Joyce. Young Children in Brief Separation (Film). 26 Washington Place, New York, NY 10003: New York University Film Library, 1976.

This series of five films and guides presents the responses of young children (ages 1-1/2 to 2-1/2 years) to separation from their mothers. Four of the children receive foster care, while one child is placed in residential nursery care. The films demonstrate how children in foster placement, who receive adequate affection and support from a substitute mother, are able to cope with their separation and trauma without accute distress and return to their own mothers with warmth and affection. The child in residential nursery care, however, does not receive adequate mothering, becomes acutely distressed, and rejects his mother at reunion.

164. Rutter Barbara A. A Way of Caring: The Parents Guide to Foster Family Care. New York, NY: Child Welfare League of America, 1978.

In most foster family situations, the needs of the parents have been neglected or even ignored. This sympathetic book is the first to answer every question parents ask or want to ask about their child in foster care. In exploring the complex, often troubling problems parents experience with

(Rutter, Barbara A.)

placement, the author enriches the understanding of placement participants and greatly enhances the opportunity for successful placement.

165. Ryan, P.; Warren, B.L.; and McFadden, E.J. Course Outline, Foster Parent Training Project. Eastern Michigan University, Department of Sociology, Ypsilanti, MI 48197, 1977. 117 pages.

The Foster Parent Training Project has available a series of courses designed for use by a project instructor in training foster parents. The courses are designed for a twenty-hour format. Each course, however, can be used as an independent unit; however, most units assume one is familiar with the introductory presentation.

166. Ryan, P.; Warren, B.L.; and McFadden, E.J. Training Foster Parents to Serve Dependent Children, Summary Progress Report. Foster Parent Training Project, Department of Sociology, Eastern Michigan University, Ypsilanti, MI 48197. 76 pages.

The extent to which the Foster Parent Training Project at Eastern Michigan University has met its proposed goals during the first two years of the project is described in this report. The report includes the progress of the first half of the 1976-77 fiscal year and outlines the plans for meeting the project goals during the fourth fiscal year.

167. Sarason, Irwin G.; Linders, Karen; and Crnic, Keith. A Guide for Foster Parents. New York: Human Sciences Press, 1976. 37 pages.

This is a useful manual for both foster parents who have already had children placed in their homes and adults contemplating doing so. It can also be used as part of the training program given by caseworkers . The Guide offers a systematic way of conceptualizing the problems in foster care, and in dealing with typical problems of adjustment, behavior, and response. There are many examples from actual foster parenting experiences to illustrate and clarify the points made.

168. Simon, Rita James, and Altstein, Howard. Transracial Adoption. New York: John Wiley and Sons, 1977. 197 pages.

In addition to reporting the outcome of research conducted by the authors, this book presents historical

(Simon, Rita James, et al)

background and literature reviews about transracial placement of Black, Asian and Indian children. Separate chapters address subsidized adoption and single-parent adoption.

169. Smith, Jerome, and Miroff, Franklin I. You're Our Child: A Social/Psychological Approach to Adoption. Washington, DC: University Press, 1981. 110 pages.

This is a book that speaks in a realistic way to the commonness of all parenting experiences and all child development struggles. At the same time it recognizes the meaning for adoptive parents and their children found in the fact that the family began legally rather than biologically. Dealing primarily with the most prevalent and traditional adoptive form, that of a healthy infant adopted soon after birth by a married couple of the same race as the child, this book reaches beyond the legalities of adoption into the social, emotional and psychological attitudes and consequences of adoption.

170. Spaulding for Children. Looking Back on Disruption (Videocassette). 3660 Waltrous Road, Chelsea, MI 48118, 1976. 60 minutes.

A panel discussion focuses on the issue of disruption in adoption placements and its effect on the adoptive parents and placement workers. It addresses these questions: What is disruption? Should workers try to save every placement? Who is to blame? What is the worker's responsibility? It stresses the need for workers to deal with their own feelings in order to help child and family.

171. Stein, Theodore, and Gambrill, Eileen. Decision Making in Foster Care: A Training Manual. 2223 Fulton Street, Berkeley, CA 94720: University Extension Publications, 1976. 228 pages.

This training manual provides step-by-step guidelines, sample charts and forms, and case examples concerning assessment and contracting, observation and recording, and intervention in parent-child interaction and in parental alcohol and drug abuse problems. It was designed for use with child welfare staff.

172. Stein, Theodore; Gambrill, Eileen D; and Wiltse, Kermit. Children in Foster Homes: Achieving Continuity of Care. New York: Praeger, 1978. 280 pages.

This report of the Alameda Project describes the intervention and results with experimental and control groups. However, the book goes beyond the reporting of research. Excellent introductory chapters provide an overview of the foster care situation. Three detailed case studies illustrate how intervention can be matched to the needs of families. The authors describe how their findings can be used by workers, supervisors, administrators and social work educators.

173. Stone, Helen D., ed. Foster Care in Question: A National Reassessment by Twenty-One Experts. New York: Child Welfare League of America, 1970.

This collection of papers presents viewpoints about many important foster care issues, including: self-concept of the foster child, preplacement treatment, and the parent-child relationship. Some of the papers are reprinted from journals.

174. Stone, Helen D., and Hunzeker, Jeanne M. Creating a Foster Parent-Agency Handbook. New York, NY: Child Welfare League of America, 1974. 48 pages.

This is a guide to the essential requirements for preparing a foster parent-agency handbook, designed to be adapted for each agency's special needs. In addition to the fundamentals of policies, rights, and responsibilities, the book includes information on foster home evaluation, keeping a child's handbook, foster parent-agency agreements, agency service evaluation, and a program guide for foster parent neighborhood groups.

175. Stone, Helen D., and Hunzeker, Jeanne M. Education for Foster Family Care: Models and Methods for Social Workers and Foster Parents. New York: Child Welfare League of America, 1974. 108 pages.

This book grew out of the CWLA project that made preservice and inservice foster parent training a nationwide pursuit. Guidelines and concepts are always accompanied by examples of existing programs that illustrate how goals can be reached in different ways under different conditions and auspices. A section on teaching of adults is particularly pertinent.

176. Tizard, Barbara. Adoption: A Second Chance. New York: Free Press, 1978. 263 pages.

Barbara Tizard challenges society's misconceptions about adoption in this British account of a group of children who spent their infancy in an institution and were then adopted, placed in foster homes or returned to their natural parents. Through extensive interviews, repeatedly conducted over a seven year period, with children and their respective adopted, natural or foster parents, Dr. Tizard and her associates found that adopted children were in a more stable situation, had fewer emotional problems, and were intellectually and academically superior to the children restored to their natural parents and to those placed in foster homes. Excerpts from these interviews provide a vivid picture of what was involved in the children's transition from institution to family home.

177. Tod, Robert, ed. Social Work in Adoption: Collected Papers. London: Longman Group, Ltd., 1971. 158 pages.

These papers about adoption, reprinted from British and American journals, span the years from 1954 to 1968. A section of four papers deals with group work with adoptive families.

178. Tod, Robert, ed. Social Work in Foster Care: Collected Papers. London: Longman Group, Ltd., 1974. 189 pages.

The editor has gathered foster care articles which appeared in American and British journals between 1952 and 1969. These collected papers, some of them classics in the field, provide an historical survey which is still relevant. One or two of these papers are dated in their approach to foster care.

179. Triseliotis, John, ed. New Development in Foster Care and Adoption. London: Routledge and Kegal Paul, 1980. 243 pages.

This collection of papers by British authors brings together recent developments in the field of foster care and adoption. It provides a helpful comparative view of solutions to problems which are common to child welfare practice in the United States as well as Britain.

180. Western Federation for Human Services, ed. Planning For Adoption (Manual). 1709 West Jefferson, P.O. Box 2526, Boise, ID 83701, n.d. 328 pages.

A collection of handbooks and resources used in placing older, physically handicapped, or mentally retarded children is presented in this adoption manual. The manual is divided into seven sections, each of which deals with a different aspect of adoption.

181. Wiltse, Kermit. Foster Care in the Seventies: A Decade of Change. P.O. Box 751, Portland, OR 97207: Regional Research Institute for Human Services, 1978. 72 pages.

This is the text of a presentation made in August, 1978 to the Third National Permanency Planning Conference. Perspectives on research and practice in foster care are presented.

4

IN-HOME SERVICES AND PARENT EDUCATION

182. Abidin, Richard R., ed. Parenting Skills: Workbook and Trainer's Manual. 72 Fifth Avenue, New York, NY 10011: Human Sciences Press, 1982. 188 page manual; 136 page workbook.

This is a complete program for parent-training workshops in a group setting. A modular approach is used covering such topics as parent and child self-images; discipline; the development of intelligence in preschool children; special education; and parental tutoring. The parent's workbook offers practical examples, exercises and assignments.

183. Agency for Instructional Television. Spoonful of Lovin' (Videocassette, Guide and Manual). Box A, Bloomington, IN 47402, 1981. Five 30 minute programs.

This set of training materials was developed specifically for day-care home providers. "A Gourmet Guide to Family Day Care" offers an overview of family day care. "Starting from Scratch" focuses on development and growth of children from birth to three. "Natural Ingredients" deals with caring for pre-schoolers and school-age children. "A Recipe for Happy Children" shows how to arrange rooms, give ideas for activities, and discusses discipline, guiding children's behavior, and when to say no. "A Measure of Good Safety" describes how to prevent accidents by childproofing cribs, choosing toys, structuring transporation, and other things in the environment. Components may be used separately or as a package.

184. American Red Cross. Parenting for Parents of Children From Birth to Two Years of Age: Group Leader Manual. 1978. 82 pages.

Contact local Red Cross Chapters for more information. This manual, stock number 321240, provides instructions and homework assignments for eight sessions of parenting classes. The sessions are: what is parenting?; safety, nutrition, and health; encouraging sensorimotor development; providing stimulation for language development and for intellectual growth; foundation of social and emotional development; discipline; and contemporary issues and problems of parenting.

185. Arch, Shirley. "Older Adults as Home Visitors Modeling Parenting for Troubled Families." Child Welfare 57 (1978): 601-605.

This article discusses the use of foster grandparents as supportive persons for families in their own homes. By acting as role models for biological parents, older persons can be an effective resource in averting child placement.

186. Armsworth, James, and Pollock, Larry. Teenage Parent Self Development Program (Manual). 600 N. Mound Street, Nacadoches, TX 75961, 1979. 236 pages.

This manual is an exercise-oriented program for use with groups of teenage parents. The life schedule approach which focuses on critical life events that teenagers must cope with is used. There is a heavy emphasis on the decision-making process. The manual can be used for sequential programmming or for planning single topics.

187. Arnold, L. Eugene and others. "Parent's Group." In Helping Parents Help Their Children. New York: Bruner/Mazel, Inc., 1978. pages 114-125.

Arnold and colleagues identify the core elements of parent groups and describe group techniques and the role of the professional in the group. Finally, different types of groups are discussed.

188 AVANCE Parent Child Education Program. Project CAN (Child Abuse and Neglect) Prevent (Curriculum, Toymaking Manual, and Slide-tape Modules). Gloria Rodriguez, Executive Director, 132 Torres, San Antonio, TX 78237, forthcoming.

This is a comprehensive curriculum on child growth and development during the formative years. Both Spanish and English versions are available. Included are outlines for class discussion, lesson plans, references, and the manual for making and using toys for child

(AVANCE Program)

growth and learning. In addition, a slide-tape presentation is being developed. Although the material has universal relevance to all children, culturally relevant issues relating to the Mexican-American are included.

189. Barnes, Beverly C., and Coplon, Jennifer. The Single-Parent Experience (Manual): 1616 Soldier's Field Road, Boston, MA 02135: Human Services Development, 1980.

The demand and advantages of being sole custodial parent are described and discussed in this model. The series helps participants recognize and deal with their feelings, provides practical information, and offers perspectives on parent-child relationships.

190. Barnett, Peter; Gaudid, Christine, P.; and Sumner, Margaret G. Parenting Children of Divorce (Manual). 1616 Soldier's Field Road, Boston, MA 02135: Human Services Development, 1980.

This workshop model is designed to help parents respond to the effect of their separation/divorce on their children, to recognize their own feelings within the process, and to strengthen the relationship between parents and child.

191. Baylor College of Medicine; Texas Child Care '76; and Gulf Regional Educational Television Affiliates. Middle Road Traveler (Film or Videocassette). Box 80699, Lincoln, NE 68501: Great Plains National Television Library, 1978. 12 reels of 30 minutes each.

This film utilizes a series of dramatic vignettes to show junior high students what they need to learn about themselves and about children before deciding to become parents. Key concepts built into the vignettes include: expectations, economics, nurturance, health, safety, discipline, legal rights and responsibilities, family living styles, nutrition, communication, interpersonal relationships and child development.

192. Bernal, Martha E., and North, Juel Ann. "A Survey of Parent Training Manuals," Journal of Applied Behavior Analysis 11 (1978): 533-544.

This is a survey of 26 commercially available parent training manuals (20 aimed at parents and 6 aimed at professionals) for use in conducting individual or group treatment. Data on each manual is compared and the little available evaluation material summarized.

193. Bornstein, Susan B. Parents of Newborns (Manual). 1616 Soldier's Field Road, Boston, MA 12135: Human Services Development, 1980.

This is a curriculum for a series of eight workshops designed to educate new parents about their infant's needs, to build their confidence in parenting, and to learn to manage competing needs and responsibilities.

194. Brazelton, T. Berry. Infants and Mothers and Toddlers and Parents. New York: Delacorte Press, 1969 and 1975. 296 and 250 pages respectively.

These two guides to child development offer engrossing examples of both the commonality among children at similar ages as well as the unique differences between individuals. Brazelton also developed the Neonatal Behavioral Assessment Scale (International Ideas, 1974).

195. Broadhurst, Diane D.; Edmunds, Margaret; and MacDicken, Robert A. Early Childhood Programs and the Prevention and Treatment of Child Abuse and Neglect. P.O. Box 1182, Washington, DC 20013: National Center on Child Abuse and Neglect, 1979. 69 pages.

This booklet, aimed at staff in the field of child care, provides an overview of child abuse and neglect and shows how staff involved in child care can help to both treat and prevent child abuse and neglect.

196. Bryce, Marvin, and Lloyd, June, eds. Treating Families in the Home: An Alternative to Placement. Springfield, IL: Charles C. Thomas, 1981. 338 pages.

This collection of papers deals with issues in the development of home-based family centered services, family assessment in the home, and service delivery in the home. The latter deals with various approaches to service delivery as well as service delivery to a variety of special client groups.

197. Bryce, Marvin and others. Placement Prevention and Family Unification: Planning and Supervising the Home Based Family Centered Program (Manual). School of Social Work at the University of Iowa, Oakdale Campus, Oakdale, IA 52319: National Clearinghouse for Home Based Services to Children and Their Families, 1980.

This manual on home based programs covers philosophy, definition, program design, supervision, and evaluation. Home based programs are family centered treatment programs aimed at helping children remain in thier homes.

198. Callard, Ester D., and Morin, Patricia E. PACT - Parents and Children Together: An Alternative to Foster Care. Wayne State University, Detroit, MI 48202: Department of Family and Consumer Resources, 1979. 166 pages.

This is a report of a project which provides intensive home based intervention service to low income families who have or are at risk of having a child placed in foster care due to inadequate parenting or an unwholesome home environment. Focus is on changing child-rearing practices and home management skills of parents in order to keep parents and children together.

199. Caplan, Frank, and Caplan, Theresa. The First Twelve Months of Life and The Second Twelve Months of Life. New York, NY: Grosset & Dunlap, Inc., 1973 and 1977. 255 and 430 pages respectively.

These companion volumes offer month by month descriptions and pictures of a child's development during his first two years. Motor development, language acquisition, social development, learning patterns, personality and psychological growth, play, and special issues are capsuled for each month of life.

200. Cassette Communications, Inc. Fathering (Audiotape). 175 Fifth Avenue, New York, NY 10010, n.d. 60 minutes.

A psychologist examines the father's role in his child's development. Included in the discussion are: the historical role of the father in the family; fathers as role models for both sons and daughters; the importance of communication in the family; discipline, homosexuality, and divorce.

201. Cooper, Grace C. Parenting Curriculum (Manual). 67 Irving Place, New York, NY 10003: Child Welfare League of America, 1973. 331 pages.

This is a set of six workbooks on child development and care for adolescent mothers. The six are "Getting to Know your Baby and Yourself/Prenatal to Birth," "Your New Human/Birth to One Month," "Learning About the World/One Month to Three Months," "Your Baby Grows/Three to Six Months," "Learning More Each Day/Six to Nine Months," and "The End of the First Year/Nine to Twelve Months." The workbooks progress to the eighth grade reading level.

202. Comer, James P., and Poussaint, Alvin F. Black Child Care--How to Bring up a Healthy Black Child in America: A Guide to Psychological and Emotional Development. New York: Simon and Schuster, 1975.

As the title states, this is a guide to psychological and emotional development of the black child in America. A question and answer format is used. Information on normal development, racial identity and self-esteem are addressed. Common concerns on childhood illnesses, peer relationships and family issues are discussed.

203. Dangle, Richard S., and Polster, Richard A., eds. Parent Training: Foundations of Research and Practice. New York: Gilford Press, 1982. c. 600 pages.

The 22 chapters describe the leading parent training programs around the country.

204. Dangle, Richard S., and Polster, Richard A. WINNING! (Multimedia). P.O. Box 32, Arlington, TX 76004: American Children's Foundation, 1979.

WINNING! consists of 22 color videotape lessons, a WINNING! specialist handbook, parent lesson guides, and WINNING! diplomas. It teaches child management skills to parents of 3--12 year olds. Participants have been voluntary, referred, and court-ordered, and include single and married parents from diverse socioeconomic groups.

205. Dimon, Vicky, and Bruer-Thompson, Cathy. Children Raising Children (Videotape). 67 Irving Place, New York, NY 10003: Child Welfare League of America, 1976. 25 minutes.

Four teenage mothers describe what it is like to be a teenage single parent. This film is useful for staff development and for discussion groups with teenage parents.

206. Dreikurs, Rudolph. Children: The Challenge and Parents' Guide to Good Discipline. New York, NY: 1964, 1970. 335 and 112 pages respectively.

These books offer a practical and supportive approach to parenting. The importance of discipline and ways of achieving it are discussed.

207. Early Childhood Program, Southwest Educational Development Laboratory. Positive Parent (T.V. spots, Booklets). 211 East 7th Street, Austin, TX 78701, 1976.

This program includes a series of television spot announcements (30 and 60 second versions) and related booklets. Each set deals with a specific parenting technique relating to discipline, language and intellectual development, social and emotional development, and family roles and relationships. T.V. spots and booklets may be used separately or together. The material was designed for a multicultural audience. It is also useful in parenting courses.

208. Education Development Center. Education for Parenthood: Family and Society Module. 55 Chapel Street, Newton, MA 02160, n.d.

This is one of a three-module training program designed to provide high school students with direct experience in working with children and in understanding the forces that shape human development. This module focuses on the effects of family and society on the growth of a child. Relevant sub-units include "Memories of Adolescence," "Under Stress," and "Raising a Family Alone." Contact the Education Development Center for more information.

209. Education Development Center. Education for Parenthood: Family and Society Module (Manual). 55 Chapel Street, Newton, MA 02160, 1979.

Significant content area and adaptation include human growth and development and the effect of family and society on the growth of a child. It was adapted for use with caseworkers through the addition of material that relates content to the worker's role.

210. Fantini, Mario D., and Cardenas, Rene, eds. Parenting in a Multicultural Society. New York: Longman, Inc., 1980. 292 pages.

This book of articles discusses ethical issues, research, and programs related to parent education and parenting in general. It also has a series of articles on special issues in parenting in various minority cultures.

211. Fiering, Alvin. Adapting to Parenthood (Film). 118 South Street, Boston, MA 02111: Polymorph Films, n.d., 20 minutes.

This film stresses the role changes which a first baby produces for both parents. It emphasizes father's roles. It includes interviews with new parents, and it shows

(Fiering, Alvin)

one young couple adjusting to the changes taking place in their lives. It should help recent parents cope with their new roles.

212. Fiering, Alvin. When a Child Enters the Hospital (Film). 118 South Street, Boston, MA 02111: Polymorph Films, n.d. 16 minutes.

This film chronicles the hospitalization of a young girl undergoing minor surgery and shows how her mother helps.

213. Footsteps (Film or Videotapes and Manual). General Services Administration, Washington, DC 20409: National Audiovideo Center, n.d.

This series of 30 parenting stories is an excellent multicultural program which has appeared on public television. "Footsteps: From A to Zach" focuses on preparing children (Zach Riley in this case) for school. Another example is "The Need for Early Stimulation, Identity, Social Skills and Competence."

214. Garbarino, James; Stocking, S. Holly; and Associates. Protecting Children from Abuse and Neglect--Developing and Maintaining Effective Support Systems for Families. San Francisco, CA: Jossey-Bass Publishers, 1980. 222 pages.

Various approaches to prevention of child abuse are discussed. Use of the family's natural helping network of friends, relatives, neighbors and others in the community are stressed.

215. Gesell, Arnold; Ilg, Frances L.; Ames, Louise Bates; and Rodell, Janet Learned. Infant and Child in the Culture of Today: The Guidance of Development in Home and Nursery School. New York: Harper and Row, 1974. 420 pages.

This classic book on child care focuses largely on the growth characteristics of infants and children. Universal levels of behavior are described by age. In addition, there are sections on individual differences, nursery school behavior and technique, and suggested toys, play materials and equipment.

216. Gifford, Carla D.; Kaplan, Felisa B.; and Salus, Marsha K. Parent Aides in Child Abuse and Neglect Programs. P.O. Box 1182, Washington, DC 20013: National Center on Child Abuse and Neglect, 1979. 57 pages.

This booklet describes how paraprofessionals can support professionals in the field of child welfare.

(Gifford, Carla D., et al)

It covers the following: what a parent aide program is; present aide-client relationships; how to develop and implement a program; training; and supervision.

217. Ginott, Haim, G. Between Parent and Child, Between Parent and Teenager and Between Parent and Teacher. New York: The Macmillan Company, 1965, 1969, and 1972. 223, 255 and 323 pages respectively.

These three books offer practical, readable advice on how to manage the day to day issues involved in child care. Full of anecdotes and sample dialogues, they offer advice on how to deal with such issues as anger, sex, communication, motivation, and setting rules and routines.

218. Gordon, Thomas. P.E.T.: Parent Effectiveness Training and P.E.T. in Action. New York: Peter H. Wyden, Inc., 1970 and 1976. 334 and 376 pages respectively.

P.E.T. is a nationwide program for parents, teachers, and others working with children. It emphasizes communication, particularly active listening skills and "I" messages, in addition to changing the environment in order to change behavior. P.E.T. offers the theory and gives examples of how the methods work. P.E.T. In Action adds to this further application and new solutions offered by parents using parent effectiveness training techniques.

219. Guerney, Louis F. Parenting: A Skills Training Manual 2d ed. P.O. Box 391, State College, PA 16801: IDEALS, 1980.

This is a manual for professionals as well as parents from all socioeconomic and educational levels. Chapters include "What parents can expect of children," "Showing understanding," "Parent messages," "Structuring," "Reinforcement," "Rules, limits and consequences," and "Putting it all together."

220. Guidance Associates. Child Development and Child Health: Nurturing the Young (Film). Communication Park, Box 3000, Mount Kisco, NY 10549, 1975.

This set of four filmstrips is designed to prepare parents-to-be for the responsibilities of caring for their growing child. "Food and Nutrition" explains why proper food and nutrition are essential to a child's healthy development. "Health and Safety" deals with "safe-proofing the home", treating common childhood illnesses, and handling emergencies. "Play and Self-Expression" explains how play encourages a child's physical and emotional development. "Love

(Guidance Associates)

and Identity" examines how children gain an understanding of what they are and form concepts of their own self worth.

221. Guidance Associates. Family Differences: Understanding Conflicts between Parents and Children (Film). Communication Park, Box 3000, Mount Kisco, NY 10549, 1977.

This series of four sound filmstrips presents an in-depth survey of how and why conflicts arise between parents and children, and provides many practical techniques for avoiding and resolving such family problems. "Daily Disagreements" enables viewers to become more aware of children's needs in daily life. "Parents Expect...Children Want..." shows how the use of rules and chores, and the allocation of time and place for play helps children become independent. "Strange New Places: Laughter or Tears?" focuses on understanding the child's behavior away from home, and preparing children for new experiences. "From Me to We: Growing Up with Others" shows viewers how to guide children's behavior and help them deal with personal relationships.

222. Guidance Associates. Growth and Development in Children A Primer for Parents (Film). Communication Park, Box 3000, Mount Kisco, NY 10549, 1974.

This set of films presents child development from infancy through age five. Included are "Prenatal Care: Preparing for Parenthood," "How an Average Child Behaves--From Birth to Age Five," "The First 18 Months: From Infant to Toddler," and "Everyday Problems of Young Children."

223. Guidance Associates. Parenting Skills: Growing Along With your Child (Film). Communication Park, Box 3000, Mount Kisco, NY 10549, 1978.

This series of four films deals with the crucial responsibilities of being a parent. The films are "Adjusting to the New Baby," "Skills for Parents," "Mother Infant Health Care," and "Child Development: The Pre-School Years."

224. Hack, Maureen. Amazing Newborn (Film). 118 South Street, Boston, MA 02111: Polymorph Films, n.d. 25 minutes.

This film is useful for child development psychology, family life, and childbirth classes as well as professionals who are helping parents prepare for and work with their babies. The film portrays the

(Hack, Maureen)

remarkable degree of behavioral development already present at birth. Three normal infants from one to seven days of age are shown reacting to visual, tactile, and auditory stimuli. The viewer is shown how to identify various patterns of behavior in infants.

225. Health Sciences Communications Center, Case Western Reserve University. Death of a Newborn (Film). 118 South Street, Boston, MA 02111: Polymorph Films, n.d. 33 minutes.

This film is intended to assist professionals in providing support to bereaved parents. It involves an interview by Dr. Marshall Klaus with the parents of a child who dies at age 28 days. The interview takes place three and one-half months later. The film shows the parents' individual grieving process, their reactions of guilt, lapses into depression, and difficulties with friends and relatives. The significance of support from professionals and the parents' need for guidance and encouragement is shown.

226. Health Sciences Communications Center, Case Western University. Dubowitz Assessment of Newborn Gestational Age (Film). 118 South Street, Boston, MA 02111: Polymorph Films, n.d. 44 minutes.

This film, clinical in nature, shows practitioners how to quickly assess a newborn's gestational age. It demonstrates the examination and scoring of a term baby and two preterm infants.

227. Hegar, Rebecca L. "Parent Education for Mexican-Americans: A Group Approach." In Parent Education for Mexican-American Child Welfare Clients. New Orleans, LA 70118: Region VI Child Welfare Training Center, Tulane University School of Social Work, 1982.

This paper gives an overview of the cognitive/small group model of parent education and discusses its use with a demonstration group of Mexican-American child welfare clients. It summarizes and assesses aspects of that group experience, and it discusses culturally relevant issues in group work with Mexican-American parents.

228. Helfer, Ray E. Child Abuse: A Plan for Prevention. 3325 Michigan Avenue, Suite 1250, Chicago, IL 60604: National Committee for Prevention of Child Abuse, 1978. 36 pages.

Dr. Helfer proposes a program of parent education and medical follow-up for all first time parents in the United States. The proposal addresses rationale,

(Helfer, Ray E.)

funding, organizational auspice, educational content, and political strategies for getting the proposal implemented.

229. Human Relations Media. Daddy Doesn't Live Here Anymore: The Single-Parent Family (Slide-tape, Cassette). Box 308, Pleasantville, New York 10570: Ibis Media, 1981. 302 slides.

This four part program is aimed at educating young people to the problems and positive features in a single-parent family. "The Changing Family" focuses on explanations for and practical aspects of divorce. "When Parents Divorce" deals with the feelings of loss and adjustment facing both children and parents of divorce. "One Day at a Time" deals with the problems of single mothers, such as money, child care, time, dating, and holidays. "The Step-Parent Family" deals with the multiple aspects involved with remarriage. Package sold as a set only, with teacher's guide.

230. Human Services Development. Parent-Teenager Communications (Film). 1616 Soldier's Field Road, Boston, MA 02135, n.d. 20 minutes.

This is a trigger film of 13 vignettes offering opportunities for parents to share experiences with each other, clarify values about teenage behavior, and practice ways to communicate with teenagers. Issues addressed include drugs and alcohol, boy-girl relations, sex, sibling rivalry, depression, suicide and delinquency.

231. Human Services Development. Parenting the Special Needs Child (Film). 1616 Soldier's Field Road, Boston, MA 02135, n.d. 25 minutes.

This trigger film of 16 vignettes depicts interactions with many of the people who affect the life of the parents of the special needs child. The film deals with the stress and stereotyping these parents face and is geared toward exploring how to cope more effectively.

232. Human Services Development. Single Parents and Their Children (Film). 1616 Soldier's Field Road, Boston, MA 02135, n.d. 18 minutes.

This is a trigger film of 13 vignettes which depicts many of the stressful situations single parents face. The purpose is to allow participants to share experiences, feelings and approaches about such issues as being with mother and father; bringing other adults into children's lives; and learning to cope with the simultaneous demands of children, work and household maintenance.

233. Human Services Development. Stepparenting Issues (Film). 1616 Soldier's Field Road, Boston, MA 02135, n.d. 20 minutes.

Thirteen vignettes present some of the emotions and situations common in families with step-parents. Some of the issues addressed include: no time alone for the new couple; having additional children; conflicts about childrearing; children attempting to come between parents; and sibling rivalry.

234. Joshua Production, Ltd. Emotional Aspects of Pregnancy (Film and Discussion Guide). 477 Roger Williams, P.O. Box 855, Ravinia, Highland Park, IL 60035: Perennial Education, Inc., 1977. 20 minutes.

Expectant parents illustrate and highlight the commonly experienced changes during pregnancy. Subjects of the film include expectant couples and one single expectant mother. Topics illustrated include intensification of emotions, doubts and conflicts about becoming a parent, changes in sexual needs, fears regarding whether or not the baby will be "normal," and changes in partner dependency.

235. Katz, David; Pierce, Robert; and Stiffman, Arlene. Normal Child Development: The First Two Years; and Normal Child Development: Two to Five Years (Videocassette or Videotape and Manual). Learning Resources Center, Campus Box 1196, Washington University, St. Louis, MO 63130: George Warren Brown School of Social Work, 1977. 25 minutes and 14 minutes respectively.

These two programs outline the major milestones of normal child development and demonstrate behaviors typical of various age levels.

236. Kempe, C. Henry. "Approaches to Preventing Child Abuse: The Health Visitor Concept." American Journal of Diseases of Children 130 (1976): 941-947.

This article identifies a set of obvservation points for prenatal and postpartum periods which help define which parents are at risk of becoming child abusers. It then proposes the use of lay health visitors to provide support for new families.

237. Laycock, Angelina; Ryan, Patricia; Warren, Bruce. Contemporary Parenting: Course Guideline for Parent Education. Eastern Michigan University, Ypsilanti, MI 48197: Institute for the Study of Children and Families, n.d.

Fourteen courses are outlined, each designed for 20 hours of classroom participation. Topics include: issues and problems in adoption; child rearing for

(Laycock, Angelina, et al)

working parents; families in transition; single parenting; step-parenting; parenting the pre-school child; parenting the school-aged child; teenagers: a challenge for parents; discipline; handling lying, dishonesty, and destructive behavior; compulsive eating and childhood obesity; helping a child move to a new home; supporting family relationships for the handicapped child; and parenting the child with mental retardation. Each unit consists of five parts. They are: general goals, specific objectives, important points, suggested activities and suggested readings and materials.

238. Levenson, Phyllis; Hale, James; Hollier, Marlene; and Tirado, Cathy. Parenting Skills: A Curriculum for Teenage Mothers (Manual). Mailing Room, The Authority for Mental Health and Mental Retardation in Harris County: P.O. Box 25381, Houston, TX 77005, 1978. 278 pages.

This parenting education curriculum for teenage mothers was designed especially for those with high-risk or handicapped babies. The curriculum was developed to teach young mothers to more effectively meet the needs of their children and to cope with the demands of their futures. Emphasis is placed on the mother's feelings, decision-making, and skills as they relate to her child's growth and development. The curriculum was designed for a twelve-week school semester and consists of twelve independent modules on the following topics: Mother's needs, child development, communication, behavior management, nutrition, health care, safety, family planning, prenatal care, and planning for the future. All information presented on child care is oriented toward ways in which teenage mothers can best stimulate their babies' physical and emotional growth.

239. Los Angeles County Department of Adoptions. Parents' Group (Film). 67 Irving Place, New York, NY 10003: Child Welfare League of America, n.d. 19 minutes.

This film depicts how an agency works with adoptive families. The group consists of parents who have had older children recently placed with them. The workers deal with the specific adjustment problems each family is having in addition to their ambivalent feelings about parenthood.

240. March of Dimes. Inside My Mom (Film or Slide Set). Box 2000, White Plains, NY 10603, n.d. 8 minutes.

This presentation illustrates through cartoon characters the nutritional needs of an unborn child. The film presents information from the perspective of a fetus as he reacts to the various kinds of food the mother eats. The nutritional value of specific foods such as cake, vegetables and milk is given. The film emphasizes the importance of the mother eating proper foods regularly, and discusses the consequences of a non-nutritional diet. A narrated cassette or record accompanies the slide set or filmstrip. The material is available in English or Spanish.

241. Maybanks, Sheila, and Bryce, Marvin, eds. Home-Based Services for Children and Families: Policy, Practice, and Research. Springfield, IL: Charles C. Thomas, 1979. 360 pages.

The proceedings of the First National Symposium on Home-Based Services, 1978, presents original papers dealing with theory, research, policy and programs relating to home-based services for children and families. The practice section includes program examples of networking, educational services, services for the developmentally disabled, health services and social services.

242. McAfee, Dralie, and Nedler, Shari. Education for Parenthood: A Primary Prevention Strategy for Child Abuse and Neglect. 300 Lincoln Tower, 1860 Lincoln Street, Denver, CO 80295: Education Commission of the States, 1976. 24 pages.

This pamphlet discusses child abuse, parent education, and prevention. It offers an overview of parent education and how it can be used to prevent child abuse.

243. Mendota Mental Health Institute. Children's Behavior in the Family (Film). Library-Media Center, 301 Troy Drive, Madison, WI 53704, n.d.

This 55" narrated videotape includes child management guidelines on the following topics: discipline, pinching and biting, personality development in children, obtaining compliance, how to ignore, scapegoating, television for children, parental moral support, fears, sibling rivalry, temper tantrums, correct use of praise, request versus command, establishing bedtime routines, modeling desired behavior, and infant care and emotional development.

244. Mendota Mental Health Institute. Family Life Styles (Film). Library Media Center, 301 Troy Drive, Madison, WI 53704, n.d.

This 55" narrated videotape explores how life styles influence childrearing. Families which are black, communal, low-income, farm, and immigrants are examined.

245. Mitchell, J. Gary, and McDonald, John. We Were Just Too Young (Film). 3710 Commercial Avenue, Northbrook, IL 60062: MTI Teleprograms, Inc., n.d. 24 minutes.

This documentary film depicts the problems of adolescent parenting and addresses the need for teenagers to deal with their sexuality in order to avoid early parenthood.

246. Morris, Larry A., ed. Education for Parenthood: A Program, Curriculum and Evaluation Guide. DHEW Publication No. (OHDS) 78-30125, Administration for Children, Youth and Families, Children's Bureau, 330 C Street, SW, Room G311, Washington, DC 20201: Behavior Associates, 1977. 179 pages.

This guide is designed to assist schools and community based organizations to develop parenthood programs and curricula for teenagers. The stated purpose is to provide general information about Education for Parenthood demonstration programs. Included are an overview of the evaluation of the programs, detailed information about materials and specific educational experiences available in reference to parenting concepts, and guidelines on how to develop and implement an Education for Parenthood program.

247. Nance, Kathy N. "Alternative Methods of Parent Education for Child Welfare Clients." In Parent Education Groups with Mexican-American Clients, edited by Rebecca L. Hegar, New Orleans, LA 70118: Region VI Child Welfare Training Center, Tulane University School of Social Work, 1982.

This article discusses a variety of alternative approaches to parent education, including various content options, goals, and organizational options. Application of these alternatives is made to the abusing and neglecting client based on an understanding of the dynamics of abuse and neglect.

248. National Center for Comprehensive Emergency Services to Children. Comprehensive Emergency Services Training Guide, 2d ed. and Comprehensive Emergency Services: Community Guide, 2d ed. Publication and Distribution Branch, 330 C Street, SW, Room G311, Washington, DC 20202: U.S.DHHS, Office of Human Development, 1976.

These materials focus upon comprehensive emergency services for families in crisis with the primary objective of preserving families intact. The Training Guide discusses the various components of a comprehensive emergency service program and their differential uses. It also provides skill development training for crisis intervention work. The Community Guide provides a step-by-step approach to the development of a comprehensive emergency service program.

249. National Clearinghouse for Home-Based Services to Children and Their Families. Home Based Family Centered Service: A Basic View (Slide-tape). School of Social Work at the University of Iowa, Oakdale Campus, Oakdale, IA 52319, n.d. 18 minutes.

This slide-tape show introduces home-based family services and depicts various situations in which it might be appropriate as an alternative to placement.

250. National Commission on Resources for Youth. The Way We See Them: Learning to Observe Infants (Film). 1 Oak Hill Drive, San Anselmo, CA 94960: Bradley Wright Films, 1981. 17 minutes.

This film shows how infants explore and learn. It won an award in the thirteenth annual NCFR film awards competition.

251. National Home Caring Council. A Better Answer (Film). 67 Irving Place, New York, NY 10003, n.d. 10 minutes.

This color film depicts homemaker-home health aide services in a variety of real life situations. It emphasizes training and supervision and the value of the service to prevent unnecessary institutionalization.

252. National Home Caring Council. A Guide to Planning, Organization, Administering a Homemaker--Home Health Aide Service. 67 Irving Place, New York, NY 10003, 1979. 250 pages.

Ten sections deal with the initiation and operation of a homemaker--home health aide program. Sections include getting started, establishing an agency, administering an agency, structuring an agency, staffing an agency, delivering services, information systems and evaluation, budgeting and financing, public relations, and a bibliography and glossary.

253. National Home Caring Council. A Model Curriculum and Teaching Guide for the Instruction of the Homemaker--Home Health Aide (Manual). Superintendent of Documents, Washington, DC 20402: U.S. Government Printing Office, 1980.

This is a basic training document. It was developed in collaboration with the American Red Cross, the American Home Economics Association, and the National League of Nursing. Ask for DHHS Publication Number HSA 80-558, GPO Stock Number 017-026-00092-5.

254. National Home Caring Council. Homefires (Film). 67 Irving Place, New York, NY 10003, n.d. 28 minutes.

This black and white film depicts one homemaker--home health aide at work with three different families facing a variety of problems.

255. National Home Caring Council. Supervision of Home Care Services (Manual). 67 Irving Place, New York, NY 10003, forthcoming.

This is a two-part curriculum--one a training guide for the instructor, the other a manual for the student. It provides information on instruction for supervisors of in-home care services--professional, paraprofessionals and volunteers.

256. National Home Caring Council. Widening Horizons--The Teaching Aspect of Homemaker Services: A Guide. 67 Irving Place, New York, NY 10003, 1974.

This volume discusses the teaching role of the homemaker and a variety of related aspects, such as how to involve individuals and families.

257. Ogg, Elizabeth. Preparing Tomorrow's Parents. No. 520, 381 Park Avenue, So., New York, NY 10016: Public Affairs Committee, Inc., 1976. 28 pages.

This pamphlet describes the need to train youth for becoming parents, and describes a number of programs which do this. It also offers tips on organizing an education for parenthood program.

258. Paget, Norman W., and Penner, G. Lewis. Family Life Education and Protective Services. P.O. Box 1266, Denver, CO 80201: American Human Association, n.d. 24 pages.

This pamphlet discusses group education and family life education in general. It also describes a small pilot voluntary parent education program, a court ordered parent education program, and the use of family life education for the protective services client in the United Kingdom.

259. Parents' Magazine Films. Developing Creative Thought in Children: Imagination at Work (Film). Communication Park, Box 3000, Mount Kisco, NY 10549: Guidance Associates, 1977.

This series of filmstrips focuses on the importance of the recognition of children's potential for creativity. Parents, teachers and other persons who frequently interact with children are told to encourage behavior which leads to the development of creativity. The series includes: 1) "Imagination and the Creative Process;" 2) "Growing Through Make Believe;" 3) "Exercises in Creativity;" and 4) "The Parents' Role in Creative Play."

260. Parents' Magazine Films. El Manana Es Hoy: A Parent Education Program (Film). Communication Park, Box 3000, Mount Kisco, NY 10549: Guidance Associates, 1978.

A parent-education audiovisual program is presented in Spanish and is designed to help Hispanic parents promote the physical, intellectual and social development of their children. It is suggested that the program be used in community agencies and parents' meetings in day care centers and schools. The program is oriented toward the overall development of bilingual/bicultural children. It recognizes the additional pressures placed on Spanish speaking families living in the U.S. The four filmstrip/tape sets include: 1) "El aprendizaje comienza en al hogar (Learning Begins at Home);" 2) "Nuestro idioma, nuestra culture, nosotros (Our Language, Our Culture, Ourselves);" 3) "Del hogar a la escuala (From Home to School);" 4) "Relaciones entre los padres y la escuala (Parent--School Relationships)."

261. Parents' Magazine Films. Mothers and Fathers: Myth and Reality (Film). Communication Park, Box 3000, Mount Kisco, NY 10549: Guidance Associates, 1977.

This filmstrip series is designed to help young parents and prospective parents become aware of the impact of a mother and father's relationship on their children, and to re-examine their roles as parents. The films are as follows: 1) "Children and Adults" explores the needs of children and examines how the quality of the mother-father relationship affects the way in which these needs are fulfilled. Also discussed are special problems faced by single parents in bringing up their children. 2) Emphasized in "Family Relationships" are five factors which greatly influence relationships between mothers and fathers and between parents and children. These are the birth of a child, the family structure, a constantly changing society,

(Parents' Magazine Films)

money and mobility, and family crisis. 3) Focusing on the parenting role, "Mother/Father Roles" explores the problems that parents face in fulfilling their responsibilities as providers and nurturers. 4) "Changes in the Family" presents concrete suggestions to parents for meeting the needs of their children in the modern world. Active participation and cooperation of parents with self-help agencies, parent groups, family counselors and government programs are encouraged.

262. Parents' Magazine Films. The School-Age Parent: A Life Begins, A Life Changes (Films). Communication Park, Box 3000, Mount Kisco, NY 10549, 1977.

This series of four sound and color filmstrips was designed to provide school age parents with information and practical assistance to help them meet the demands of parenthood. The accompanying discussion guide and audio script booklet are included to assist in the utilization of the following films: 1) "Becoming a Parent: The Emotional Impact;" 2) "Dealing with Practical Problems of Parenthood;" 3) "Rights and Opportunities;" and 4) "Building a Future." It is suggested that these filmstrips would be useful for guidance, family life, and parenthood classes in junior high schools, senior high schools, colleges and universities.

263. Parents' Magazine Films. Understanding Children 6-12: The Forgotten Years (Films). Communication Park, Box 3000, Mount Kisco, NY 10549: Guidance Associates, 1978.

This filmstrip is designed to help parents and care-givers understand the importance of middle childhood and the role they can play in encouraging a child's healthy development. The filmstrips suggest that, by maintaining open channels of communication, parents can help children cope with the changes of middle childhood and make those years enjoyable to all. 1) "A Sense of Self" examines the developmental accomplishments which parents can expect during middle childhood, with emphasis on the level of social, emotional and intellectual maturity needed to function successfully in society. Also considered are the factors which influence a child's development of his/her self-image and how adults can contribute to the development of a healthy one. 2) Examined in "Physical Development" is the impact of the physical changes that occur during middle childhood upon a child's emotional, social and intellectual growth. 3) "The Growth of Intelligence" stresses the need for parents to encourage a child's interests and learning abilities between the ages of 6 and 12. 4) the focus in "The Child and the Family"

(Parents' Magazine Films)

is on how family relationships change as school, peer groups, and the desire for independence increase in importance during the child's middle years. 5) "The School Experience" explores the role of parents and teachers in providing a complete educational experience for children.

264. Parents' Magazine Films. When A Child Dies (Film). 135 West Wells Street, Milwaukee, WI 53202: National Funeral Directors Association, 1981. 23.5 minutes.

This film deals with the experiences of parents after a child dies. It presents interviews with three bereaved couples. The film provides a rare glimpse into the aftermath of what is considered to be the most devastating psychological blow a human being can suffer.

265. Rambasek, Patricia E. The Ties that Bind (Film). 118 South Street, Boston, MA 02111: Polymorph Films, n.d. 27 minutes.

This film portrays how relationships between parents and infant are experienced in pregnancy and during and immediately after birth. It suggests ways to improve interaction between parent and infant through speech, gesture, touch, scent, and paying attention to the baby's cues.

266. Riley, Donald P.; Apgar, Kathryn; and Eaton, John. Parent-Child Communication (Manual). 1616 Soldier's Field Road, Boston, MA 02135: Human Services Development, 1977.

This is a guide for conducting parent-child communication workshops. Drawn from family life education experiences of the Family Services Association of Greater Boston, the workshop is aimed at developing listening skills in parents, encouraging sensitive means of expression, teaching problem-solving techniques, and creating an opportunity to encourage the discussion of individual concerns.

267. Smith, Judith M., and Donald, E.P. Child Management: A Program for Parents. Michigan: Research Press, 1966. 97 pages.

This is a self-instruction booklet for parents and other child care specialists aimed at child management. It deals specifically with consistency in parental behavior, using rules to provide consistency and create a comfortable environment.

268. Soyka, Patricia. Thursday's Child Has Far To Go: Help at Home for Handicapped Children and Their Families. 67 Irving Place, New York, NY 10003: National Home Caring Council, 1979.

This book shows how homemaker-home health aides can help preserve the home and family when they are confronted with children with special problems.

269. Spock, Benjamin McLain. Baby and Child Care. New York: Pocket Books, 1961. 666 pages.

The past several generations have been reared with the aid of this classic guide. While it addresses the psychological impact on the parent of having a baby, it is most commonly used as a guide to the physical care of infants and children. There is also considerable information on age-related child development. Topics vary from clothing, feeding, illnesses, and first aid to traveling with a baby.

270. Sundel, Martin, and Homan, Carolyn Clark. "Prevention in Child Welfare: A Framework for Management and Practice." Child Welfare LVIII (1979): 510-521.

This article differentiates primary prevention from early intervention and treatment and rehabilitation in child welfare. It provides examples of service activity for a number of child welfare related problems at each of these three levels of intervention.

271. The University of Michigan School of Social Work. Prevention and Work with Natural Helpers (Videotape, Audiotape, Study Guide). 1015 East Huron, Ann Arbor, MI 48109: Child Welfare Learning Laboratory, 1976.

This program emphasizes the use of informal and semi-formal helpers in social work and introduces the idea that prevention should be aimed at the person at risk. This is one of six in a series of training modules designed for use with child welfare line service workers.

272. Urban Rural Systems Associates. Everyone Needs A Parent: A Curriculum in Parenting Training (Manual). Superintendent of Documents, Washington, DC 20402: U.S. Government Printing Office, n.d.

This 10 unit (20 1/2 hour total) curriculum is aimed at: 1) exploring different attitudes regarding parenting and classifying values; 2) increasing awareness of the effect of personal interactions on the development of children; and 3) reinforcing the concept of differential rates of development of children and how crucial parental expectations are regarding development. It provides exercises and resources, and offers good appendix material on developmental growth, and planning a group.

5

INSTITUTIONS AND SPECIAL NEEDS CHILDREN

273. Adessa, Sylvester, and Laatsch, Audrey. "Therapeutic Use of Visiting in Residential Treatment." Child Welfare 44 (1965): 245-251 and 261.

The authors state, on the basis of their experience with a residential treatment program, that parental visits have a therapeutic value, but can be sufficiently stressful to be counter-productive; consequently, they give guidelines for making visits as beneficial as possible for children and parents.

274. Albert, Stuart W., and Starr, Philip. "A Family-Centered Approach to the Treatment of Emotionally Disturbed Children in Placement." The Forum for Residential Therapy 2 (1971): 397-403.

The authors discuss a family-centered approach that they developed in a residential treatment center for the emotionally disturbed child. The focus of the approach is to assist the family in accepting the child's separation and the child's life away from the family.

275. Children's Home Society of Cincinnati. Education Services (Videotape). 5051 Duck Creek Road, Cincinnati, OH 45227, 1976. 5 minutes.

This brief videotape describes the educational services available to children and youth at the Children's Home Society in Cincinnati, a residential treatment center. The tape is intended for use as a staff development tool and should help to stimulate thought and discussion regarding the subject of educational services within the context of a residential treatment center.

276. Children's Home Society of Cincinnati. Greg and Mrs. Walz (Videotape). 5051 Duck Creek Road, Cincinnati, OH 45227, 1976. 5 minutes.

This videotape presents some of the prescriptive components of residential treatment facility placement for adolescents. It depicts a 14-year-old boy, Greg, who was admitted to the facility when he was 12 years old. He describes some of his school, personal and family problems. Greg's mother describes her search for help for her son and the beneficial outcome of the placement. The film gives a presentation of the use of behavior modification and casework in a group living setting and an interpretation of residential treatment services.

277. Children's Home Society of Cincinnati. Gwen (Videotape). 5051 Duck Creek Road, Cincinnati, OH 45227, 1975. 5 minutes.

This videotape depicts 13-year-old Gwen in a residential treatment center. She has been in placement for eight months and is now ready for discharge to her father. She talks about why she was placed at the center and how the staff helped her find solutions to her problems. The tape is intended for staff development purposes.

278. Children's Home Society of Cincinnati. Positive Peer Culture (Videotape). 5051 Duck Creek Road, Cincinnati, OH 45227, 1976. 30 minutes.

This videotape presents a service approach used in a residential treatment facility for adolescents. The team leader of the positive peer culture program describes the PPC principles. This tape is designed to complement the videotape "Billy M." It is useful for staff development purposes to illustrate the PPC approach.

279. Children's Home Society of Cincinnati. Ray (Videotape). 5051 Duck Creek Road, Cincinnati, OH 45227, 1976. 60 minutes.

This videotape focuses on an adolescent's adjustment to placement in a residential treatment facility. Early in the film, Ray discusses his referral to the Children's Home. Then the film depicts an interview held six months later in which Ray talks about his problems and about the program at the center. This is intended to use in staff development and for evaluation of service programs.

280. Costin, Lela B. The Training of Personnel for the Licensing of Family Homes in Child Welfare. Washington, DC: DHHS, 1965. 218 pages.

This three year demonstration project to train non-professionals for licensing day care and foster homes was a cooperative venture between a school of social work and ten state divisions of child welfare. It was stimulated by concern about manpower shortages and the need for new approaches to training nonprofessionals in social work positions.

281. David, Anthony; Ryan, Richard; and Salvatore, Peter. "Effectiveness of Residential Treatment for Psychotic and Other Disturbed Children." American Journal of Orthopsychiatry 38 (1968): 469-475.

The findings of this study support the need for participation of parents in the treatment process. An important finding is that the child is more apt to remain in his home following discharge if there has been active parental involvement during residential treatment.

282. Dickerson, Martha Ufford. Fostering Children with Mental Retardation. Ypsilanti, MI: Foster Training Project, Eastern Michigan University, MI 48197, 1977. 182 pages. Instructor's manual, 95 pages. Trainee's manual, 95 pages.

This is a comprehensive training program for foster parents providing basic understanding of the behavioral experiential program.

283. Finkelstein, Nadia Ehrlich. "Children in Limbo." Social Work 25 (1980): 100-104.

The author reviews the plight of children left in limbo in a variety of foster care situations. The importance of comprehensive services to children and their families to prevent or quickly terminate their placement in an uncertain status is stressed.

284. Finkelstein, Nadia Ehrlich. "Family-Centered Group Care." Child Welfare 59 (1980): 33-41.

The author examines the ways of changing residential care. Alternatives for family-centered group care that focus on work with the family and are intended to achieve a permanent discharge goal as quickly as possible are presented.

285. Finkelstein, Nadia Ehrlich. "Family Participation in Residential Treatment." Child Welfare 53 (1974): 570-575.

This article states that it is crucial to involve the biological parents of the child in placement by showing respect, flexibility and awareness of strengths. If this is done, the residential stay will be appreciably shortened.

286. Fochios, Stephen. "The Use of Families and Family Members as Therapeutic Levers in Treatment of Disturbed Delinquent Children." Child Welfare 44 (1965): 556-562.

This article describes a treatment program at a halfway house for delinquent boys who have been ready to prepare for an eventual return home. The program stresses the role of parents in treatment and includes techniques aimed at involving the family.

287. Gitelson, Paul. "A Model to Avoid the Institutionalization of Children." Journal of Sociology and Social Welfare 6 (79): 805-813.

The concept of "deinstitutionalization" has led to a great deal of concern being focused on moving children out of large institutions into community based programs. This article proposes a model program that would seek to avoid the initial placement of the child and focus attention on working with the family as a total unit.

288. Guidance Associates. Behavioral and Emotional Disabilities (Filmstrip with Tape Cassettes). Communication Park, Box 3000, Mount Kisco, NY 10549, 1975.

This filmstrip reviews patterns for behavior symptomatic of many types of emotional disorders, including such severe problems as autism, negativism, and withdrawal. The selected treatment programs for emotionally disturbed children covered are play therapy, art/music/dance therapy, drug therapy, and behavior modification.

289. Guidance Associates. Educational and Language Disabilities (Filmstrip with Tape Cassette). Communication Park, Box 3000, Mount Kisco, NY 10549, 1975.

This filmstrip presents the educational and language disabilities that can occur when there is a breakdown in any part of the language cycle: hearing, processing in the brain, speech and feedback. It is emphasized that language disorders are not self-contained handcaps; they affect nearly every aspect of a child's development. It is also stressed that an early and accurate diagnosis is essential for treatment.

290. Guidance Associates. Intellectual Disabilities (Filmstrip with Tape Cassette). Communication Park, Box 3000, Mount Kisco, NY 10549, 1975.

In this filmstrip, the problems of dealing with mild mental retardation are discussed. Three types of educational intervention programs are covered: social learning, perceptual-motor training and language training. The filmstrip stresses that, in order to adequately help a mentally retarded child, parents must understand the child's condition, learn more about themselves, and seek the appropriate sources of outside help.

291. Guidance Associates. Physical Disabilities (Filmstrip with Tape Cassette). Communication Park, Box 3000, Mount Kisco, NY 10549, 1975.

This filmstrip presents the problems facing the physically disabled child. The psychological and practical problems of the physically disabled child and the caregiver are covered. The great importance of focusing treatment on the individual child's needs, rather than trying to force the child to conform to an existing treatment program, is stressed.

292. Hammond, John W. "Child Care Workers As Helpers to Parents." Child Care Quarterly 2 (1973): 282-284.

The author describes the specific ways in which child care workers in a residential setting seek to help parents.

293. Heiting, Kenneth H. "Involving Parents in Residential Treatment of Children." Children 18 (1971): 162-167.

This article reviews the development of a program involving the boy's parents in the treatment process of a residential treatment center. The program shortened the duration of the placement and allowed for the return of most boys to their own homes. The problem of uninvolved parents is also addressed.

294. Katz, David; Pierce, Robert; and Stiffman, Arlene, Blindness (Videocassette). George Warren Brown School of Social Work, Washington University, St. Louis, MO 63130, 1977. 15 minutes.

This videocassette begins with an opthamologist explaining the definition of blindness and the importance of early identification and treatment of it. The tape presents two case histories in which families and children discuss their actual experiences with blindness.

295. Katz, David; Pierce, Robert; and Stiffman, Arlene. Cerebal Palsy (videocassette). George Warren Brown School of Social Work, Washington University, St. Louis, MO 63130, 1977. 22 minutes.

In this tape, cerebal palsy is defined and explained, as well as procedures for diagnosis and treatment. The tape presents two case histories in which families share their experiences in coping with children having cerebal palsy.

296. Katz, David; Pierce, Robert; and Stiffman, Arlene. Deaf-Blind (Videocassette). George Warren Brown School of Social Work, Washington University, St. Louis, MO 63130, 1977. 16 minutes.

This tape presents the parents of a three-year-old deaf-blind child discussing their attempts to face the reality of raising their multiply handicapped child. The tape also focuses on the child, illustrating characteristics of the deaf-blind.

297. Katz, David; Pierce, Robert; and Stiffman, Arlene. Deafness (Videocassette). George Warren Brown School of Social Work, Washington Unniversity, St. Louis, MO 63130, 1977. 17 minutes.

An audiologist defines the two types of hearing loss, as well as the variability of deafness. The process of educating the deaf child is presented. The tape presents two families discussing their feelings and reaction to their child's deafness.

298. Katz, David; Pierce, Robert; and Stiffman, Arlene. Diabetes (Videocassette). George Warren Brown School of Social Work, Washington University, St. Louis, MO 63130, 1977. 23 minutes.

A physician defines diabetes and its symptoms. Two cases are discussed. The first case concerns the parents of a five-year-old who present their reactions to the discovery of their child's diabetes. The second case is a nineteen-year-old diabetic who reminisces about his reactions to having diabetes.

299. Katz, David; Pierce, Robert; and Stiffman, Arlene. Learning Disabilities (Videocassette). George Warren Brown School of Social Work, Washington University, St. Louis, MO 63103, 1977. 23 minutes.

A physician defines and explains learning disabilities, stressing that identification is difficult because these children many times appear normal. Three case histories are presented in which mothers describe their children's learning disabilities.

300. Katz, David, Pierce, Robert; and Stiffman, Arlene. Mental Retardation (Videocassette). George Warren Brown School of Social Work, Washington University, St. Louis, MO 63130, 1977. 25 minutes.

The tape begins with a social worker who has a specialty in mental retardation defining the symptoms and forms of mental retardation. Two cases are presented. The first concerns parents discussing their child's mental retardation. The second is about a family discussing the problems they are faced with in dealing with their child's mental retardation.

301. Katz, David; Pierce, Robert; and Stiffman, Arlene. Parents' Reaction to Handicap (Videocassette). George Warren Brown School of Social Work, Washington University, St. Louis, MO 63103, 1977. 16 minutes.

An expert discusses the typical development phases parents undergo in accepting a child's disability. The professional's role in helping and guiding the parents into fully accepting their child's handicapped condition is presented.

302. Koret, Sydney. "Family Therapy as a Therapeutic Technique in Residential Treatment." Child Welfare 52 (1973): 235-246.

The author describes a residential program which utilizes family therapy as a part of treatment. Problems are seen in systems terms and parents are actively involved in the problem-solving process. The article sees family therapy as an important adjunct, specifically in crisis intervention and in helping the child to consolidate treatment gains during return to the family.

303. Korty, John, and Couturis, Bill. Can't It Be Anyone Else? (Film). 3801 Colorado Avenue, Santa Monica, CA 90404: Pyramid Films, 1982. 30 minutes.

This film introduces three children who have been stricken with leukemia, the most common form of cancer to afflict children. Through the exploration of the children's reaction to the harsh realities of their disease, the viewer is shown the wisdom, insight and wry humor that these children use in confronting their problems. This film can be used as a training device to provide increased understanding about children who have leukemia.

304. Kreech, Florence. "A Residence for Mothers and Their Babies." Child Welfare 54 (1975): 581-592.

The author describes a residence for unwed mothers and their babies. Particular emphasis is placed on the delineation of the roles of staff members.

305. Krona, David A. "Parents as Treatment Partners In Residential Care." Child Welfare 59 (1980): 91-96.

The author discusses and illustrates various ways of involving parents in the treatment of their emotionally disturbed children.

306. Lamson, Amy. Psychology of Juvenile Delinquency. New York: Human Sciences Press, 1982. 160 pages.

This book draws a distinction between the sociological pressure related to delinquency and the psychological characteristics associated with the juvenile offender. Case examples are presented and treatment strategies are suggested. This text should be useful for the classroom or for use in in-service training of professionals working with the juvenile delinquent.

307. Langer, Sydney. Scared Straight? Fear in the Deterrence of Delinquency. Washington, DC: University Press of America, 1981. 140 pages.

This is an evaluation of the effectiveness of the Juvenile Awareness Program ("Scared Straight") of the Lifer's Group of Rahway Prison in the deterrence of juvenile delinquency. This book explores the evolution of the program, provides a graphic description of the encounter session, and concludes with the therapeutic effects of the program.

308. Letulle, Leslie J. "Family Therapy in Residential Treatment for Children." Social Work 24 (1979): 49-51.

The author elaborates on the historical progression of "exclusion to inclusion" of families from the 1940's to the 1950's and 1960's in treatment of children placed in residential facilities. The primary emphasis is on the positive impact of family therapy in residential treatment facilities. The author also covers concepts that are applicable to work with parents and children in foster care.

309. Littauer, Celia. "Working with Families of Children in Residential Treatment." Child Welfare 59 (1980): 225-234.

The author examines in detail and illustrates the many ways in which child care workers can help families of children in residential centers to facilitate early return home. Child care workers can be effective by encouraging family involvement in cottage life, modeling, providing direct help to parents, and participating in after care service.

310. Magnus, Ralph A. "Teaching Parents to Parent: Parent Involvement in Residential Treatment Programs." Children Today 3 (1974): 25-27.

The author believes that parental involvement is an important ingredient to successful treatment and suggests concrete ways to increase the participation of parents in residential treatment programs.

311. Mandelbaum, Arthur. "Family Process in the Diagnosis and Treatment of Children and Adolescents." Bulletin of Menninger Clinic 35 (1971): 153-166.

The author suggests that the use of family process in conjunction with other treatment methods when a child has been placed in a residential facility will benefit the parents, the child, and staff. The author feels that the refusal of the family to be involved may be due to absence of a consistent conceptual approach to family process.

312. McClintock, Donald R. "Involving Parents in Solving a Group Problem in Residential Treatment: A Case Report." Child Care Quarterly 4 (1975): 44-47

This article illustrates through a case example, the impact of family involvement in successful residential treatment.

313. Mendota Mental Health Institute. Home and Community Treatment: Activating Family Change (Film). Library Media Center, 301 Troy Drive, Madison, WI 53704, 1976. 32 minutes.

This film demonstrates an intermediate approach between customary outpatient or residential treatment modalities. The focus is on an interdisciplinary team approach for the treatment of emotionally disturbed children and their families. The film follows a family through treatment, depicting the innovating therapeutic approach developed by the Home and Communith Treatment Program of the Mendota Mental Health Institute.

314. Meyer, Margaret. "Family Ties and the Institutional Child." Children 16 (1969): 226-231.

The author describes a residential setting where 80% of the children will stay until they complete high school. The author feels that involving the family in the preplacement process will increase the likelihood that the child will accept placement. If the natural families are not involved, the institution provides foster families who will provide the child with a stable adult relationship while in placement.

315. Moss, Sidney Z. "Integration of the Family into the Child Placement Process." Children 15 (1968): 219-224.

This article discusses the process of family-centered casework as a treatment method in residential settings. The family, rather than the child, is the focus of treatment. The child's pathology is seen as a part of the family's pathology. The family is viewed as the unit of treatment.

316. MTI Teleprograms, Inc. Dead End (Film). 3710 Commercial Avenue, Northbrook, IL 60662, 1978. 12 minutes.

This film is designed for both professionals and youths. The film reviews the career of Judge Joe Sorrentino, a lawyer and part-time judge in the Los Angeles Juvenile Court. Sorrentino is show interacting with young people already in the criminal justice system and speaking to adult groups on the problems of the system in an attempt to effect improvements.

317. MTI Teleprograms, Inc. Delinquency: Prevention and Treatment (Film). 3710 Commercial Avenue, Northbrook, IL 60662, n.d. 20 minutes.

This film explores three current delinquency treatment and prevention programs: police diversion, peer-pressure therapy, and community corrections. The film raises some thought-provoking viewpoints and questions about current prevention and treatment programs.

318. MTI Teleprograms, Inc. Nobody Cuddled Bobby (Film). 3710 Commercial Avenue, Northbrook, IL 60662, 1978. 14 minutes.

This film is designed for a range of audiences which includes professionals. It examines the juvenile detention system through the story of a seventeen-year-old youth who had a record of minor crimes and status offenses. The child is described by his parents as incorrigible and he is sent to a correctional

(MTI Teleprograms, Inc.)

Institution at the parents' request to "teach him a lesson." This child hangs himself four and one-half months later in prison after being raped by adult inmates.

319. MTI Teleprograms, Inc. Precinct 94-142 (Film). 3710 Commercial Avenue, Northbrook, IL 60662, 1981. 22 minutes.

The objective of this film is to develop awareness about the reasons why communication often breaks down among physicians, educators, and parents as they work toward early identification, and potential referral of handicapped children. The film also focuses on stereotypes and attitudes about the handicapped child.

320. MTI Teleprograms, Inc. Squires of San Quentin (Film). 3710 Commercial Avenue, Northbrook, IL 60661, 1978, 30 minutes.

This film is about a volunteer intervention project in which San Quentin inmates interact with juvenile delinquents from communities in northern California. The film features the development of relationships between youths and the convicts. The purposes of the Squires program, as illustrated in the film, are to demonstrate the consequences of criminal behavior, to show the "quicksand" effect of entering the justice system, to motivate community groups to develop counseling programs and related services for young people, and to serve as a model in the development of special programs for in-need young people.

321. MTI Teleprograms, Inc. The Reluctant Delinquent (Film). 3710 Commercial Avenue, Northbrook, IL 60662, n.d. 24 minutes.

This film examines the high correlation between learning disabilities and juvenile delinquency. It is designed to heighten awareness and increase the understanding of all people concerned with the problem of juvenile delinquency. This film focuses on a case history of what can be done to help young people with undiagnosed learning disabilities and to divert them out of the criminal justice system.

322. Oxley, Genevieve B. "Involuntary Clients' Responses to a Treatment Experience." Social Casework 58 (1977): 607-614.

The author suggests that the successful treatment, discharge and subsequent positive functioning of boys in residential treatment is contingent upon

(Oxley, Genevieve B.)

the mandatory involvement of the natural parents in counseling sessions. The boys and their parents are viewed as involuntary clients, since neither requested treatment. Practice sessions are offered for working with involuntary clients.

323. Riley, Donald P.; Eaton, John; and Lippman, Daniel. Growing With Your Learning Disabled Child. Boston, MA: Human Services Development, 1980.

This small book can be utilized for conducting workshops for parents who have children with learning disabilities. It can be used in helping parents to understand what learning disabilities are and to discover ways they can support their learning disabled child's growth and development.

324. Roberts, J., and Lynch, M. "The Treatment of Abused Children and Their Families." Social Work Today 8 (1977): 10-12.

The authors describe a residential unit in a British hospital that provides assessment and treatment of abused children and their families through a multidisciplinary approach.

325. Rogan, Edward F. "The Family Rehabilitation Program." Child Welfare 49 (1970): 464-472.

The author discusses and evaluates a program modeled on the "halfway house" concept with the rehabilitation and reunion of the family as key goals. A variety of disciplines and services were utilized to reunite parent and child.

326. Romig, Dennis A. Justice for Our Children. Lexington, MA: Lexington Books, 1978. 206 pages.

This state-of-the-art report on the juvenile justice system examines the successes and failures of various rehabilitative approaches. This book discusses why the system has failed to help youths and ways to improve on treatment programs and the system as a whole. It also covers the treatment modalities currently employed by workers in the juvenile justice system including casework, behavior modification, individual therapy, and family therapy.

327. Schoen, Mark. Sara Needham: A Special Person (Film). Focus International, 1776 Broadway, Suite 508, New York, NY 10019, 1981. 30 minutes.

This film details the life experiences of Sara Needham who was born without legs and one arm. It portrays her emotional strength, adaptations, and her sexual adjustment. Also discussed is the lifestyle she has had to develop for herself.

328. Smith, William C. Reactions to Delinquency. Washington, DC: University Press of America, 1978. 144 pages.

This text discusses the social organization of delinquency and the decision making apparatus of the juvenile justice system. It should be useful for training professionals in how to function effectively in this system.

329. Texas Department of Human Resources. A Visit With Norris Class on Day Care (Videocassette). P.O. Box 2960, Austin, TX 78769: Media Services Division, n.d. 27 minutes.

Norris Class, a noted authority on child care licensing, discusses his philosophy of licensing. He is interviewed by two day care licensing education directors.

330. Texas Department of Human Resources. Norris Class on Institutional Licensing (Videocassette). P.O. Box 2960, Austin, TX 78769: Media Services Division, n.d. 30 minutes.

Institutional licensing team leaders talk with Norris Class, noted authority on child care and licensing, about standards and philosophy. This tape is intended for institutional licensing representatives.

331. Thornton, William E.; James, Jennifer A.; and Doerner, William G. Delinquency and Justice. Glenview, IL: Scott, Foresmand and Company, 1981. 544 pages.

This text provides an overview of the extent, causes, nature and control of juvenile delinquency in the United States. It examines the major theories and research on delinquency and delinquency-control programs and provokes though, discussion and debate. It can be adapted to both classroom teaching and in-service training of professionals.

332. Trieschman, Albert E.; Whittaker, James K.; and Brendtro, Larry K. The Other 23 Hours: Child Care Work With Emotionally Disturbed Children in a Therapeutic Milieu. Hawthorne, New York: Aldine Publishing Company, 1969. 256 pages.

This text deals with the treatment of emotionally disturbed children in the residential setting. Covered are suggestions about major routines of the child's day, as well as recommendations about games, activities, observation procedures, and the pitfalls to be avoided.

333. University of Missouri. Manual for Instructors: Service to the Mentally Retarded Youth Offender. 8011 Natural Bridge Road, St. Louis, MO 63131, 1973. 84 pages.

This small text provides a curriculum guide for an orientation to the characteristics of retarded youthful offenders and methods of working with them. It is designed for use in a variety of settings and by different groups including social workers. Emphasis is on educational programs.

334. Washington Research Project, Inc. Children in Adult Jails. Washington, DC: Children's Defense Fund, 1976. 77 pages.

This small text focuses on the subject of children placed in adult jails. It cover the physical conditions of these jails, the type of adult criminals with whom these children are placed, the medical attention received by the children, the recreational facilities available, and the age and sex of the children. Actual interviews of the children are also included.

335. Weber, George H. Child Menders. Beverly Hills, CA: Sage Publications, 1979. 223 pages.

This book focuses on the problems of treating institutionalized delinquents. A series of cases in the format of vignettes are provided for workshop use. This book is designed for those working with youth or preparing to work with youth.

336. Whittaker, James K., and Trieschman, Albert E., eds. Children Away From Home: A Sourcebook of Residential Treatment. Hawthorne, New York: Aldine Publishing Company, 1972. 455 pages.

The editors of this book are committed to the philosophy of treating the child in the life milieu. The first part of the book concerns the current problems and issues of residential treatment. The second part deals with the treatment of the emotionally disturbed child in the residential setting.

6

MINORITY CLIENTS

337. Adams, Bert. Kinship in an Urban Setting. Chicago, IL: Markham Publishing Company, 1968.

This book describes a major strength of the black family as its ability to extend itself to non-biological definitions of the family unit.

338. Baird, Cynthia, ed. LaRaza Films: A List of Films and Filmstrips. Oakland, CA: Latin American Library, Oakland Public Library, 1972. 68 pages.

This is a listing of films and filmstrips on Mexican-Americans.

339. Baker, Cynthia Christy. A Resource Guide to Work With American Indian and Spanish Speaking Clients. New Orleans, LA: Region VI Child Welfare Training Center, Tulane University School of Social Work 70118, 1981. 17 pages.

The resource guide includes annotated entries on audio-visual and multimedia packages, handbooks and audio materials. The material provides a compiled list of materials available for use in work with American Indian and Spanish speaking clients who reside in the Southeast.

340. Baker, Cynthia Christy. Work with Urban Black Families. New Orleans, LA: Region VI Child Welfare Training Center, Tulane University School of Social Work 70118, 1981. 81 pages.

This manual was developed for classroom teachers and child welfare agency trainers. It contains exercises, course outlines, teaching modules, and bibliography listings. It also includes a unit on methods and techniques for presenting minority content.

341. Baurley, Marion E., and Street, Matthew H. American Indian Law: Relationship to Child Abuse and Neglect. Washington, DC: U.S. Government Printing Office, 1981. 56 pages.

This report reviews American Indian Law relating to child abuse and neglect. It provides general background information about this developing area of law, and it presents a framework which can be used to analyze individual child welfare cases which involve Indian children. The three types of court systems used by various tribes are described and an appendix notes which tribes use which type of system. Another appendix includes a series of tables which present important features of 51 tribal codes.

342. Billingsley, Andrew. Black Families in White America. Englewood Cliffs, NY: Prentice-Hall, Inc., 1968.

This book uses the social systems approach to demonstrate the interdependence of black families with other levels of society. The variability of black family forms, the subsystem of the larger society that impact on family life, and the subsystem of the black community and black family are discussed.

343. Billingsley, Andrew. "Family Functioning in the Low-Income Black Community." Social Casework 50 (1969): 563-572.

This is a literary review on the black family which analyzes the structure of the black family and its relationship to poverty among low-income blacks. The information shows strong kinship bonds, mutual aid networks and other strengths.

344. Billingsley, Andrew, and Giovannoni, Jeanne M. Children of the Storm: Black Children and American Child Welfare. New York: Harcout, Brace & Jovanovich, Inc., 1972.

The position of black children in the American child welfare system is reported from an historical perspective.

345. Bowles, D. "Making Casework Relevant to Black People: Approaches, Techniques, Theoretical Implications." Child Welfare 48 (1969): 468-475.

Social casework techniques and methods are examined for their applicability to black people. Suggestions are given on specific methods for engaging and working with black clients.

346. Brown, Eddie F., and Gilbert, Betty B. Social Work Practice with American Indians: A Schema for Identification and Inclusion of American Indian Content into the Social Work Curriculum. Tempe, AZ 85281: American Indian Projects for Community Development Training and Research, Arizona State University, School of Social Work, 1978. 66 pages.

This is a narrative which outlines and identifies major content on Indians which should be included in social work curricula. General areas, as well as the family and child welfare, are accompanied by a bibliography.

347. Brown, Eddie F., and Shaughnessy, Timothy F. Education for Social Work Practice with American Indian Families: Introductory Text. Tempe, AZ 85281: American Indian Projects for Community Development Training and Research, Arizona State University, School of Social Work, 1978. 77 pages.

These materials provide a basic course book for understanding the history, religion, customs, culture and lifestyles of American Indians. Practice issues are covered in terms of Indian needs and not based on the larger society's needs. The textbook is accompanied by an instructor's manual.

348. Cheek, Donald. Assertive Black...Puzzled White: A Black Perspective on Assertive Behavior. San Luis Obispo, CA: Impact Publishers, Inc., 1976.

Assertiveness training for the black population is the focus of this book. The material contained gives specific points for working with black clients. Exercises and information for the non-minority trainer are included.

349. Chicano Training Center, Inc. A Model Course Syllabi Compendium: Social Work and Chicano Content. 3520 Montrose, Suite 216, Houston, TX 77006, 1978. 222 pages.

This is a compendium of course syllabi designed to incorporate Chicano content into social work education. Course content focuses on social work practice, human behavior and the social environment, and policy, planning and administration.

350. Chicano Training Center, Inc. Curriculum Schema. 3520 Montrose, Suite 216, Houston, TX 77006, n.d.

The Curriculum Schema contains ten modules for training mental health personnel and social service workers in values of the Chicano culture. Actual training is provided by Chicano Center staff. It involves seminar,

(Chicano Training Center)

institute and workshop formats and varies in duration from two to four days. The Schema contains a syllabus with a descriptive summary of the content of each module. The modules are grouped around the major themes of "Heritage," "Identity," and "Family and Community Lifestyles." As noted, this training product is designed to be presented by the staff of the Chicano Training Center. Requests regarding training should be directed to the Center.

351. Chicano Training Center, Inc. Proceedings of the Texas-New Mexico Symposium on the Delivery of Mental Health Services to Mexican-Americans. 3520 Montrose, Suite 216, Houston, TX 77006, 1978.

This report contains the proceedings of a symposium designed to enhance mental health service delivery to Mexican-American clients. It includes presentations by recognized practitioners in mental health settings on issues such as underutilization of mental health services by Mexican-Americans and innovative approaches to addressing this problem. A transcript of a panel discussion on legislation related to the mental health needs of Chicanos includes techniques to develop meaningful contacts with state legislative bodies regarding mental health planning and program needs.

352. Children's Bureau. Child Abuse, Neglect and the Family Within a Cultural Context. Washington, DC: U.S. Government Printing Office, 1978.

This report examines cultural issues related to the identification and treatment of child abuse and neglect.

353. Children's Home Society of Cincinnati. Single Parent Adoption (Videotape). 5051 Duck Creek Road, Cincinnati, OH 45227, 1976. 30 minutes.

This videotape portrays a black single woman who has adopted a child. She discusses the problems she is encountering as a single, working adoptive mother. The videotape is intended for use as a staff training tool.

354. Citizens' Committee for Children of New York, Inc. In Search of Safe Haven: Foster Care Programs for Unaccompanied Indochinese Refugee Minors in New York. 105 East 22nd Street, New York, NY 10010, 1980. 70 pages.

This document provides a comprehensive review of the New York foster care program for Vietnamese refugee children who are unaccompanied by parents. The study

(Citizens' Committee for Children)

began in 1979. It is one of the few resources available about foster care for Asian children.

355. Cross, Andrea. "The Black Experience--Its Importance in the Treatment of Black Clients." Child Welfare 53 (1974): 158-166.

The use of community, cultures, and experience in the black environment is discussed. The need to keep the client's background and heritage always present is emphasized.

356. Devore, Wynetta, and Schlesigner, Elfriede. Ethnic-Sensitive Social Work Practice. St. Louis, MO: C.V. Mosby Co., 1981. 285 pages.

This book deals with concepts basic to understanding ethnic groups and their cultures. It deals with black, Mexican-American, Indian and European immigrant cultures in the discussion of the needs for ethnic-sensitive practice.

357. Flynn, Barbara, and others. Chicano: A Selected Bibliography of Materials. Riverside, CA: Riverside Public Library, 1971. 92 pages.

This is a list of materials about Mexican-Americans. It includes sections on culture, lifestyles, and history, along with references and resource materials.

358. Gomez, E.; Jennings, D.E.; and Santos, Y., eds. Selective Guide to Materials Related to the Chicano for Human Service Training and Education. San Antonio, TX: Worden School of Social Services, Our Lady of the Lake University, 1976. 251 pages.

The guide is designed to promote and facilitate the skillful selection and use of Chicano-relevant educational materials in human service training and social work education. The following subjects are covered: aging; Chicano movement; culture; drug use and abuse; education; folk medicine; health; language; marriage and family; mental health; and social welfare.

359. Good Tracks, Jim G. "Native American Noninterference." Social Work 18 (1973): 30-34.

This article deals with social work and intervention and practice with Indian populations. It focuses on the problems and interference sometimes caused by inappropriate intervention.

360. Goodman, James A., ed. Dynamics of Racism in Social Work Practice. Washington, DC: National Association of Social Workers, 1973. 357 pages.

This is a collection of thirty articles divided into four groups. The setting (cumulative psychological effects of racism); treatment (problems/hopes blacks and whites experience); community organization (knowledge and skills needed); and professional education (effects of racism on curriculum). The focus is on therapeutic encounters between blacks and whites in the client worker relationship.

361. Green, James W., and Tong, Collin, eds. Cultural Awareness in Human Services (Manual). Seattle, WA: University of Washington School of Social Work, Center for Social Welfare Research, 1979. 442 pages.

Skills relevant to cross-cultural social work are discussed. Topics include: developing an ability to identify the needs and priorities of ethnic minority clients; sensitivity to value and cultural differences between the worker and the client; awareness of modes of intervention with minority clients; and general characteristics of minority communities and families.

362. Hegar, Rebecca L, and Rodriguez, Loyda. Permanent Planning for Mexican-American Children in Foster Care: A Handbook Supplement. New Orleans, LA 70118: Region VI Child Welfare Training Center, Tulane University School of Social Work, 1982. 116 pages.

This training manual supplements the Oregon Project Handbook for Social Workers by Pike and others. It provides a guide to culturally sensitive services to Chicano foster children and their families. Introductory readings concern: family patterns, cross-cultural placements, language and literacy issues, mental health evaluation and treatment, religious issues, migrant families, and undocumented aliens. One chapter provides a guide for trainers.

363. Hill, Robert Bernard. The Strengths of Black Families. New York: Emersom Hall Publishers, 1972.

The book identifies and discusses the five basic strengths found in black families: 1) strong kinship bonds, 2) strong work orientation, 3) adaptability of family roles, 4) high achievement orientation, and 5) religious orientation. This book may be used in social work practice for understanding the positive aspects of black families.

364. Hopps, June G., ed. Social Work 27 (1982): 1-120.

This is a special issue of Social Work entitled "Social Work and People of Color." It provides basic general information on the concept, context and current status of people of color. This volume also deals with policy issues; and finally, it addresses social work practice with a variety of minority groups.

365. Ladner, Joyce A. Tomorrow's Tomorrow: The Black Woman. Garden City, NY: Doubleday and Co., Inc., 1971.

The black woman in American society is described according to socialization, self-image, and historical perspectives. The material clearly depicts the role of racism and social forces in the development of the black woman.

366. Landau, Hortense R., and others. "Court Proceedings Involving Indian Children" in Child Protection: The Role of the Courts (USER Manual Series). Washington, DC: National Center on Child Abuse and Neglect, DHHS, 1980.

This manual briefly addresses work under the Indian Child Welfare Act. It covers jurisdiction, legal procedures, placement preferences, records, tribal courts and notice to parties.

367. Lewin, Linda. Growing Up Indian (Film). 228 West 16th Street, New York, NY: Benchmark Films, 1981. 22 minutes.

This film illustrates aspects of the lives of two adolescent Indians living on their reservations. Insights into the special identities of these Mohawk and Cherokee youths are shared.

368. Martin, Elmer P., and Martin, Joanne Mitchell. The Black Extended Family. Chicago, IL: The University of Chicago Press, 1978.

The extended family system in the black population has both historical and current relevance to the development and survival of black families. This book looks at black family patterns and networks.

369. McAdoo, Harriet Pipers. Black Families. Beverly Hills, CA: Sage Publications, 1981. 303 pages.

This is a collection of articles that is divided into sections on 1) conceptualization of the black family; 2) demographic characteristics; 3) attitude toward "pair bonding;" 4) socialization in black families; 5) black family policies and advocacy.

370. Montalvo, Frank F.; Lasater, Tonia T.; and Garza, Nancy. A Mexican-American Culture Simulator for Child Welfare: Teaching Modules and Trainer's Manual. San Antonio, TX: Office of Continuing Education in Human Services, Worden School of Social Service, Our Lady of the Lake University, 1981. 84 pages and 200 pages respectively.

This training module consists of 2 volumes of 20 vignettes each and a training manual provides an introduction to cross-cultural counseling with Hispanic clients, an extended discussion of the culture and practice, implications of each incident, references, outline of Hispanic and Anglo-American values, and a glossary of terms. A training kit, containing these items plus test materials, selected reference monographs, and visual aids, is also available.

371. Montoya, Jose R. Cultural and Ethnic Awareness Manual for Professionals Working with Mexican-American Families. P.O. Box 917, Laredo, TX: Texas Migrant Council, Inc., National Resource Center on Child Abuse and Neglect for Mexican-American Migrants, 1980. 58 pages.

Developed for agency trainers and social work educators, this manual contains six units which include: Mexican-American history, cultural awareness, Mexican-American family, traditional medical approaches, situations affecting migrant families, and migrant child welfare.

372. National Broadcasting Corporation. The Navajo Way (Videocassette or Film). 1144 Wilmette Avenue, Wilmette, IL 60091: Films, Inc., 1975. 52 minutes.

Interwoven in the story of Mary Grey Mountain, her son, Robert Lee, and aged medicine man, Long Salt, is the story of the People--the Navajo. This largest of American Indian tribes has survived within the white man's society because of its complete involvement with tradition, the Navajo "way." The Navajo adapt, as when Long Salt goes to the white man's clinic for treatment, but they do not change; Long Salt returns to his family for ancient healing ceremonies before he considers himself well again. Without ignoring the problems of poverty, of disease, or alcoholism, The Navajo Way is a sensitive film reflecting the spiritual life of a proud community. As long as they remain Navajo, retaining their culture, their dignity and pride, and their firm belief in themselves, the People will survive and flourish.

373. National Indian Child Abuse and Neglect Resource Center of NACT. Training Materials: Native American Coalition of Tulsa. 6539 East 31st Street, Suite 1, Tulsa, OK 74135, 1980.

This resource material is a collection of papers which are available individually or as a package. The collection deals with issues related to native American experience. The package includes:
1) "Behavioral Characteristics of Domestic Violence;"
2) "Communication Skills;"
3) "Familial Incest;"
4) "Forms and Indicators of Institutional Abuse;"
5) "Implementing the Indian Child Welfare Act;"
6) "Indian Culture and Its Relationship to Child Abuse and Negelct;"
7) "Low Prognosis Categories;"
8) "The Extended Family and Its Relationship to Parenting;"
9) "The Home Visit;" and
10) "The Social Worker and the Indian Client."

374. National Resource Center on Child Abuse/Neglect for Mexican-American Migrants. La Mujer eL Amor, y eL Miedo (Film). P.O. Box 917, Laredo, TX, n.d. 20 minutes.

This film shows why abuse occurs in the migrant community. In addition, the feelings that men and women have toward abusive situations are discussed.

375. Parents' Magazine Films. With Pride to Progress: The Black Child (5 Filmstrips, 3 Tape Cassettes). Communication Park, Box 3000, Mount Kisco, NY 10549: Guidance Associates, 1979.

These filmstrips suggest ways in which black parents can help their children develop personal pride and a sense of identity with their culture. They consider the need for the black child to gain knowledge of his history and culture. The films are accompanied by audioscript booklets and a discussion guide.

376. Parents' Magazine Films. With Pride to Progress: The Chicano Child (5 Filmstrips, 3 Tape Cassettes). Communication Park, Box 3000, Mount Kisco, NY 10549: Guidance Associates, 1976.

Focusing on family and community life, this filmstrip shows how the Chicano child can experience conflict between traditional values and Anglo-American values and culture. Positive aspects of the Chicano child's heritage and culture are given. The package also includes audioscript guides and a discussion booklet.

377. Parents' Magazine Films. With Pride to Progress: The Indian Child (5 Filmstrips, 3 Tape Cassettes). Communication Park, Box 3000, Mount Kisco, NY 10549: Guidance Associates, 1976.

This package demonstrates the Indian child's behavior, shows traditional values, parent-child roles and cultural conflicts. Audioscript booklets and a discussion guide are included.

378. Parents' Magazine Films. With Pride to Progress: The Puerto Rican Child (5 Filmstrips, 3 Tape Cassettes). Communication Park, Box 3000, Mount Kisco, NY 10549: Guidance Associates, 1976.

This set examines the effects of Puerto Rican culture on the development of the Puerto Rican child and explores how traditional beliefs and values can both contribute to and conflict with healthy development. A view of three generations of a Puerto Rican family is given to show contrasts.

379. Region VIII Child Abuse and Neglect Resource Center. National Indian Child Conference (18 Audiotapes). 1205 Oneida, Denver, CO 80220, n.d.

These tapes include a collection of conference tapes and materials. They are: The Two Worlds of the Indian Child; Keeping Families Together; Exploring Parenting; Overall Development of Indian Children; Alcohol and the Newborn; Critical Issues in Early Education of Indian Children; Helping the Abused Child; and The Power of Positive Identity.

380. Region X Child Abuse and Neglect Resource Center. A Curriculum in Cross-Cultural Awareness for Human Services Workers. 156 Yesler Way, Suite 208, Seattle, WA 98104, n.d.

This series of lecturettes, exercises and group materials was designed for training caseworkers in cultural awareness and cultural differences/likenesses for practice with minority clients.

381. Sager, C.J.; Braybog, T.L.; and Waxenberg, B.C. "Black Patient--White Therapist." American Journal of Orthopsychiatry 42 (1972): 415-423.

Black client--white therapist interaction and issues are explored in the therapeutic setting.

382. Scanzoni, John A. The Black Family in Modern Society. Boston: Allyn and Bacon, Inc., 1971.

This is a report in which black fathers and mothers share family history and life experiences that contributed to their success. Strong parental functionality and high achievment motivation are factors explored in the review of strengths of the black family.

383. Screenscope, Inc. Black Girl (Videotape). 3600 M. Street, N.W., Suite 204, Washington, DC 20007, 1980. 29 minutes.

This is an adaptation of the Broadway play of the same title. The videotape deals with the tensions and jealousies that exist when one girl tries to escape from the destructive influences of her unemployed and unfulfilled sisters.

384. Shoshoni Productions. The Hopi Way (Film). 1144 Wilmette Avenue, Wilmette, IL 60071: Films, Inc., 1972. 22 minutes.

The Hopi have occupied land on three Southwestern mesas for 1300 years. They have lived in harmony with nature and themselves, shunning most efforts at assimilation into society. The movement of a large coal mining company into the Black Mesa area now threatens to upset this life. The reaction of both young and old to this invasion is negative; most Hopis want to preserve their way of life.

385. Slaughter, E.L. Indian Child Welfare: A Review of the Literature. 2142 South High Street, Denver, CO 80208: Center for Social Research and Development, Denver Research Institute, University of Denver, 1976.

The material covers significant literature published on Indian child welfare before 1976. Legal issues, reservation versus non-reservation Indians, and tribal handling of child abuse and neglect are covered.

386. Sotomayor, M. "Language, Culture and Ethnicity in Developing Self-Concept." In Life Span Development. Edited by Martin Bloom, pages 50-55. New York: The Macmillan Co., 1980.

The role of language, culture and ethnicity are addressed in terms of their effect on the self-concept. Issues of self-esteem and identity are covered.

387. Texas Department of Human Resources. Everybody Needs A Forever Home (Film). Media Services, P.O. Box 2960, Austin, TX 78769, 1976. 20 minutes.

This film focuses on black adoption, particularly older sibling groups. Adoptive families discuss feelings, expectations, problems and joys. It is intended for staff development and adoptive parent recruitment.

388. Texas Migrant Council, Inc. Child Abuse and Neglect Slide Presentations (Slides, Film, Audiocassettes). P.O. Box 917, Laredo, TX 78040, 1977.

These Too Are Americans. These slides depict the culture and lifestyle of the Mexican-American migrant farmworkers, showing the life situation and problems encountered by migrant workers as they travel through the migrant cycle. 25 minutes.

T.M.C. Migrant Child Abuse and Neglect Prevention Project. These slides tell the story of T.M.C.'s three year research and demonstration project. They depict the environment of migrant farmworkers where the potential for neglect is great. They show the possible avenues for addressing the problem of abuse and neglect in the migrant farmworkers' community. 25 minutes.

My Father, My Brother and Me. In this film, Paco, the retarded son of a migrant worker, strays from home and gets lost. The father, afraid that the police might take his son from him, refuses to ask for police help in finding Paco. Meanwhile, the police locate Paco and charge the father with child neglect. The case finally comes to trial with lawyers, police officers, social workers and Paco's sister and father all arguing about what would be best for Paco. 28 minutes.

The Texas Migrant Council in Action: The Child Abuse and Neglect Project (Slides-Audiocassette). The special problems faced by migrant workers and how their problems contribute to child abuse and neglect are discussed. Such relief measures as the establishment of day care centers and parent-run child abuse councils are covered. Speakers include representatives of the Texas Department of Human Resources and staff members of the Texas Migrant Council who were once migrant workers themselves.

389. Texas Migrant Council, Inc. Training Curriculum for Child Protective Service Workers. P.O. Box 917, Laredo, TX 78040, 1980.

This curriculum consists of five parts: 1) a brief summary of the historical development of the Mexican-American people in the Southwest; 2) a portrayal of the contemporary Mexican-American family; 3) a presentation of the unique cultural characteristics found in the lifestyle of migrant families; 4) a review of traditional approaches to health and religion. The fifth section examines the present state of existing migrant child welfare services and reviews some of the barriers that impede migrant participation.

390. University of Texas at Austin. Service Delivery for Mexican-American Children (Multimedia). P.O. Box 2960, Austin, TX 78769: Media Center, Texas Department of Human Resources, 1978. 27 minutes.

This is a training package designed for use with caseworkers of the Texas Department of Human Resources who work with Mexican-American families. It contains three training modules, each requiring half-day training sessions. The modules are entitled, "The Hispanic Culture of America," "The Mexican-American Community," and "The Mexican-American Family." Emphasis is placed upon understanding and appreciating Mexican-American culture, breaking down cultural stereotypes, and understanding family and community structures. Caseworkers are encouraged to use resources within the barrio (community) when attempting to assist families and to be aware of the cultural implications of various service delivery issues and approaches. Eight handouts, educational and director's guide and coursebook are included.

391. U.S. Department of Health and Human Services. A Selected Bibliography on Black Families. Washington, DC: Government Printing Office, Office of Human Development, 78-30140, 1978.

A review of significant child welfare materials published on the black family is given in this selected bibliography. Annotations of books, articles and resource materials are listed.

392. Washington University. Racial and Cultural Rejection (Videotape). St, Louis, MO 63130: George Warren Brown School of Social Work, 1976. 10 minutes.

Racial and cultural rejection of social workers by clients are depicted. Scenes show clients refusing to cooperate with the worker due to racial or cultural bias and mistrust.

393. Wilcox, Preston. Making Social Work Relevant to Black People: A Bibliography. New York: Afram Associates, Inc., 1970.

Preston Wilcox gives annotations about materials which include: social policy, history, practice and community issues for social workers. This is designed for agency and school training.

394. Wilson, Ames N. The Developmental Psychology of the Black Child. New York, NY: Africana Research Publications, 1978. 216 pages.

This book provides a selection of topics related to black child development. Topics include health and nutrition, socialization, cognitive development, and personaltiy development.

7

TRAINING AND INTERVIEWING METHODS

395. Ballen, Julius R.; Salus, Marsha K.; and Winett, Sheila. Supervising Child Protective Workers. P.O. Box 1182, Washinton, DC 20013: National Center on Child Abuse and Neglect, 1979. 48 pages.

This training manual offers a conceptual framework for carrying out supervisory functions effectively. The manual focuses on building a foundation for effective service delivery, on the role of supervision in a child protective service unit, on skills and techniques for supervising workers, and on information and skills needed to cope with special staff needs in a child protective service environment.

396. Broadhurst, Diane D., and MacDicken, Robert A. Training In the Prevention and Treatment of Child Abuse and Neglect. P.O. Box 1182, Washington, DC 20013: National Center on Child Abuse and Neglect, 1979. 68 pages.

This training manual concerns the importance of training in the identification, reporting, diagnosis, treatment and prevention of child abuse and neglect. It focuses on the following issues: why training in the prevention and treatment of child abuse and neglect is vital; when training should be conducted; who should train and who should be trained; what is the training program design; and how readily available are resources to assist the trainer.

397. Continuing Education Program in Human Services. Staff Development for Supervisors (Handbook and Workbook). University of Michigan School of Social Work, 1105 East Huron, Ann Arbor, MI 48109, 1977. 174 pages and 123 pages respectively.

(Continuing Education Program)

This training package is designed for us by supervisors who have staff development responsibilities. Issues such as role of the supervisor in staff development process, contracting with staff, and conducting needs assessment are covered.

398. Danish, Steven; D'Augelli, Anthony; Haver, Allen; and Conter, Jane. Helping Skills. New York: Human Sciences Press, 1980.

This is a unique training program designed to enhance the helping skills of volunteer workers, paraprofessionals, and human service personnel. The authors provide a detailed approach to developing the following skills: increasing awareness of one's own motivation to be a helper; vitalizing effective verbal and non-verbal behavior; understanding the communication of others; using effective self-involving behavior; and establishing optimal helping relationships. Included with the program are a trainer's workbook as well as a leader's manual.

399. Dukettee, Rita. Structured Assessment: A Decision-Making Guide for Child Welfare. 300 South Wacker Drive, Chicago, IL 60606: DHHS, Region V, n.d. 20 pages.

This self-instructional guidebook provides a step-by-step decision making approach for the child welfare worker who must decide whether or not to remove a child from his/her home. It covers four general criteria for measuring the need for placement and includes key questions which the worker can raise during the interview process.

400. EPD Consortium C. Expanding Services Through Volunteers (Slide-Tape). P.O. Box 2960, Austin, TX 78769: Texas Department of Human Resources, Media Services Division, 1978. 23 minutes.

This slide-tape provides a step-by-step approach to developing a volunteer program within the child welfare and juvenile justice related agencies. It can be used to help staff overcome resistance to a volunteer program and to teach staff how to supervise volunteers.

401. EPD Consortium C. The Realities of Adolescent Care: Staff Training (Slide-Tape). P.O. Box 2960, Austin, TX 78769: Texas Department of Human Resources, Media Services Division, 1978.

This training package is designed to enhance the knowledge and skills of child welfare workers,

(EPD Consortium C)

supervisors, and administrators who work with adolescents in need of alternative care. The package consists of eight modules: 1) recruitment of foster parents, 2) selection and evaluation, 3) expanding services through volunteers, 4) selection of house parents, 5) supervision of foster parents, 6) supervision of house parents, 7) contracts, a method for maintaining placement, and 8) adolescent growth and development.

402. Gambrill, Eileen D., and Stein, Theodore J. Supervision in Child Welfare: A Training Manual. Berkeley, CA: University of California, 1979. 225 pages.

The purpose of this training manual is to offer practical guidelines to child welfare supervisors which will maximize their efforts in assuring the effective delivery of services to clients. It is also intended that the materials presented will be beneficial to line workers in handling their cases more effectively and monitoring progress more carefully.

403. Garrett, Annette. Interviewing 2d ed. New York: Family Service Association of America, 1972. 209 pages.

This is a basic text for teaching interviewing to human service workers. The text is divided into two parts which include the nature of interviewing and illustrative interviews. A variety of case examples are presented which provide problems encountered in interviewing.

404. Gelfano, Bernard; Starak, Igor; and Nevidon, Patricia. "Training for Empathy in Child Welfare." Child Welfare 53 (73): 595-600.

This article reports on an innovative training program for child welfare workers designed to improve performance in empathy and concreteness. The program, based on association exercises and dyadic interchange with peer and trainer feedback, produced promising results.

405. Goldstein, Harriet. "The Effective Use of Volunteers in Home-Based Care." In Home Based Services for Children and Families. Edited by Sheila Maybanks and Marvin Bryce, pp. 237-259. Springfield, IL: Charles C. Thomas, Publisher, 1979.

This chapter discusses the problems and issues involved in operating a volunteer program in the delivery of

(Goldstein, Harriet)

home-based services. The main focus is on using volunteers as a resource, their task assignments and their recruitment. The author also covers briefly how to implement and sustain a volunteer program.

406. Guidance Associates. Cooperation Among Family, Staff and Community (Filmstrip with Tape Cassette). Communication Park, Box 3000, Mount Kisco, NY 10549, 1978.

This training package emphasizes that cooperation is the key to success of any child care program. It illustrates how home visits, telephone conversations, and formal and informal conferences are techniques for establishing a worker-parent relationship. It also stresses the need for close communication among personnel to provide effective services.

407. Jones, Martha L. "Developing Training Resources for Permanency Planning." Children Today 9 (1980): 25-26.

This article discusses the development of three training manuals for workers and supervisors developed by the Training Resources in Permanent Planning project at Millersville State College, Pennsylvania. The manuals were field tested and found effective in helping staff in the areas of setting more permanent plans for children in care, achieving more goals with clients, and in having fewer emergencies in their case loads.

408. Kadushin, Alfred. The Social Work Interview. New York: Columbia University, 1972. 337 pages.

A book designed to train professionals to interview. Major topics presented are: 1) communication and relationships, 2) the phases of the interview, 3) cross-cultural interviewing, 4) nonverbal communication, 5) the group interview. Case examples are presented illustrating problems confronted in the interviewing process.

409. Katz, David; Pierce, Robert; and Stiffman, Arlene. Basic Counseling Skills (Videocassette). George Warren Brown School of Social Work, Washington University, St. Louis, MO 63130, 1977. 49 minutes.

The purpose of this training package is meant to demonstrate basic counseling skills in attending, classification, and self-expression. Models of desirable counselor behavior are presented for the purpose of having learners practice these skills. The package includes three training modules.

410. Katz, David; Pierce, Robert; and Stiffman, Arlene. Intervention Skills (Videocassette). George Warren Brown School of Social Work, Washington University, St. Louis, MO 63130, 1977. 124 minutes.

This training package is meant for the beginning direct service worker. The materials highlight the structure of such worker-directed activities as referral taking, the initial interviewing, and assessment. Simulated case situations are presented. Trainees are encouraged to critique the worker's behaviors presented and to consider what their own response might be. Nine different modules are part of this training package.

411. Katz, David; Pierce, Robert; and Stiffman, Arlene. The Social Worker's Role: Preliminary Assessment and Referral (Videocassette). George Warren Brown School of Social Work, Washington University, St. Louis, MO 63130, 1977. 21 minutes.

The tape presents the social worker's role through dramatized situations in which a worker performs preliminary assessment and referral in the case of a suspected development problem. A home visit is conducted in which the worker gathers information on the child, observes the child's behaviors, and initiates a medical referral.

412. Katz, David; Pierce, Robert; and Stiffman, Arlene. Training (Videocassette). George Warren Brown School of Social Work, Washington University, St. Louis, MO 63130, 1976. 41 minutes.

This training package is meant for agency staff-development and managerial personnel. It presents basic concepts and techniques used by trainers to analyze tasks and develop programs for training. This training package consists of four training modules.

413. Katz, David; Pierce, Robert; and Stiffman, Arlene. Utilizing Closed-Circuit Television for Training (Videocassette). George Warren Brown School of Social Work, Washington University, St. Louis, MO 63130, 1976. 39 minutes.

The purpose of this training package is to introduce closed-circuit television as a training device for staff developers. It introduces the viewer to the basic hardware of a small television system and the logic of its use. This package shows how a trainer can use videotape to expose workers to situations they may encounter in practice. It also includes two training modules.

414. Lauffer, Armand. Practice of Continuing Education in the Human Services. New York: McGraw-Hill, 1977. 227 pages.

A comprehensive overview of continuing education programs (CEP) in the human services is presented. The Lauffer team focuses on what staff developers and educators are doing, how they're doing it, and why they are doing it. Developing trends in continuing education are pinpointed.

415. Lauffer, Armand, and Gorodezky, Sarah. Volunteers. Beverly Hills, CA: Sage Publications, 1977. 80 pages.

This guide discusses the many ways in which providers of human services may extend or expand their programs through the use of volunteers. Also examined are the pros and cons of working with volunteers in various situations and the tasks involved in developing a volunteer program.

416. Learning Resources Corporation. Situational Leadership Film (Film). 8517 Production Avenue, San Diego, CA. 16 minutes.

This film gives a visual presentation of the situational leadership model. It is designed for individuals in leadership/management/supervisory positions and is adaptable as a learning tool for the humand services organization.

417. Maluccio, Anthony N. "Staff Development in Child Welfare: A Review of Recent Literature." Child and Youth Services 1 (1977): 1-9.

This article reviews and summarizes pertinent findings in the literature with particular focus on "goals, programs, innovations, effectiveness and issues" of importance to staff development over the last ten years. Particular attention is given to the gaps in the literature, such as cost effectiveness and funding, and to other concerns that need further exploration in relation to such issues as staff development and in-service training programs.

418. Mannheimer, Joan. "Adapting Nonprofessional Skills to Coordinate Agency Volunteer Services." Child Welfare 46 (1967): 305-309.

This article presents a discussion of the effective use of volunteers. The author feels that the supervision of volunteers is an administrative function, not a casework function. The coordination of volunteers may be best accomplished through the employment of a community relations worker with the skills and experinece to direct a volunteer program.

419. MTI Teleprograms, Inc. Interviewing the Abused Child (Film). 3710 Commercial Avenue, Northbrook, IL 60662. 21 1/2 minutes.

Through a series of actual and recreated interviews, children of various age levels, subjected to different types of abuse, are seen and heard as professionals talk with them about their abuse experiences. This film is designed as a training tool for teaching how to interview the abused child.

420. National Center on Child Abuse and Neglect. We Can Help! A Curriculum on Child Abuse and Neglect (Multimedia). P.O. Box 1182, Washington, DC 20013, 1979.

This is a basic curriculum for multidisciplinary groups. The curriculum contains: Introduction to Child Abuse and Neglect; Abuse; Neglect; Emotional Maltreatment of Children; Sexual Abuse; Child Protection Intervention; The Role of the Courts; Community Planning; and Coordination to Prevent Abuse and Neglect. Audiovisual materials are included.

421. National Center on Child Abuse and Neglect. We Can Help! Specialized Training for Protective Service Workers (Multimedia). P.O. Box 1182, Washinton, DC 20013, 1979.

The curriculum consists of six training units in the area of child abuse and neglect and is designed for child protective service workers. Total training time is approximately 37 hours. The unit includes: Introduction to Child Abuse and Neglect; Identification Sequence; Conducting the Investigation; Case Management; The Social Worker in Court; and Community Organization. Audiovisual materials are included.

422. National Institute for Advanced Studies. Comprehensive Syllabus for a Child Welfare Training Program. Washington, DC: DHHS, 1980.

This is a comprehensive syllabus intended to help in the development of a curriculum to provide basic skills to child welfare staff. It includes various training modules on working with biological families.

423. Naylor, Harriet H. Volunteers Today: Finding, Training and Working with Them. New York: Association Press, 1967. 192 pages.

This book stresses the need for volunteers in human service agencies. The author presents concrete and specific ideas and suggestions. It is translated from educational and personnel administration techniques and methods and should be useful for involving and training the new volunteer.

424. Pennsylvania Department of Public Welfare. Developing Performance Standards: Supervisor's Handbook. Office of Manpower, Departmental Manpower Annex, P.O. Box 2675, Harrisburg, PA 17120. 34 pages.

This is a self-instructional guide which provides supervisors with information and materials to develop performance standards through the use of objective techniques. This handbook provides a brief overview of management objectives and exercises in writing task analyses and performance standards. Also included is a sample job description and guidelines for conducting performance evaluations.

425. Phelan, Joseph F. "Developing New Professional Categories of Volunteers in Child Welfare Services." Child Welfare 45 (1966): 214-217.

This article discusses the need for volunteers in the delivery of child welfare services. The author suggests that the use of volunteers enriches and expands the existing services to meet community needs. The author feels that the use of volunteers increases the understanding and support between the child welfare services agency and community, thus giving both of them a purpose in the spectrum of social welfare needs.

426. Pippin, James A. Developing Casework Skills. Beverly Hills, CA: Sage Publications, 1980. 158 pages.

This book covers concerns related to the caseworker and client. The component parts of the helping relationship are presented. The text has a short chapter on the social work interview. This chapter covers the interviewing process and provides information on the role of communication in interviewing.

427. Regional Institute of Social Welfare Research, Inc. The Case Management Model (Videocassette). Heritage Building, P.O. Box 152, Athens, GE 30603, 1977. 55 and 38 minutes.

This training package presents a case management model designed to serve as an organizing principle and procedural guide for the delivery of social services to the public sector. The package covers evaluation of service request or need; eligibility of determination; planning; arrangement; provision; overseeing; and recording. Training manuals are included.

428. Rich, John. Interviewing Children and Adolescents. New York: MacMillan Company, 1968. 119 pages.

This is a basic text which focuses on interviewing children and adolescents. The issues covered concern: communication, assessment and recording, the interviewing room, and observing children. Several case examples are presented.

429. Schindler-Rainman, Eva, and Lippitt, Ronald. The Volunteer Community. 2d ed. San Diego, CA: University Associates, Inc., 1975. 176 pages.

This is a book designed for staff involved in the training of volunteers. The authors offer an introductory chapter on democracy and volunteerism; summarize current trends affecting volunteerism; review the emerging changes in this field; explore the motivational bases for volunteerism; summarize the problems and practice of recruitment and orientation of volunteers; and elaborate on the roles and functions of administrators of volunteer programs.

430. Schubert, Margaret. Interviewing In Social Work Practice: An Introduction. New York: Council on Social Work Education, 1971. 86 pages.

This monograph covers the various aspects pertinent to the interview and gives insight into the techniques used in applying this method. It is designed for the beginner in the field. Problems the social worker might encounter are also covered.

431. Schulman, Eveline D. Intervention in Human Services. St. Louis, MO: C.V. Mosby Company, 1974. 235 pages.

This book is a general text appropriate for training human service workers. The text is divided into four parts: 1) the basis for human services; 2) the what and how of interviewing; 3) the parts of the interview; and 4) from interviewing to counseling. An extensive glossary of defining terms relevant to interviewing is provided.

432. Scott, Robert A., and Houts, Peter S. Individualized Goal Planning in Social Services. Milton S. Hershey Medical Center, Pennsylvania State University, Hershey, PA 17033, 1978. 125 pages.

This training manual is designed to provide staff with the necessary skills to develop meaningful social service goals and to organize plans to achieve these goals. The manual is divided into five sessions where participants learn techniques on how to motivate clients to develop, achieve and maintain meaningful

(Scott, Robert A., et al)

goals through the use of service contracting principles. The manual can be used by trainees to conduct training sessions or can serve as a self-instructional tool for agency workers.

433. Shulman, Lawrence. Skills of Supervision and Staff Management. Itasca, IL: F.E. Peacock Publishers, Inc., 1982. 384 pages.

This book focuses on the communications, relationships, teaching and group leadership skills needed by supervisors and administrators in order to help their staff work more effectively. Presented are models of supervision that are designed to help supervisors understand how to implement their complex human relations task. A large number of specific, detailed examples of supervisors in action, dealing with practical day-to-day problems, are included.

434. Shulman, Lawrence. Social Work Practice Behavior in Two Child Welfare Agencies (Videocassette). Film Rental Center, Syracuse University, 1455 East Colvin Street, Syracuse, NY 13210, 1982. 107 minutes.

This is a two part presentation. Part 1 describes nine behavior groupings presented to an audience of social work students: contracting, elaborating client's concern, empathic responses, the demand for work, providing data, dealing with systems, identifying obstacles to work, sharing workers feelings, and dealing with endings. Part 2 presents a study of the relationship between these nine behaviors and a number of outcome measures. Questionnaires designed to measure social work behavior and client satisfaction are described.

435. Stenzel, Anne K., and Feeney, Helen M. Volunteer Training and Development. rev. ed. New York: The Seabury Press, 1976, 204 pages.

The recruitment, training and educational development of volunteers are presented in this manual. It was designed for those planning to set up volunteer programs in various types of agencies and organizations, for directors of volunteers who wish to improve their administrative skills, and for staff members who want to learn more about the problem-solving and educational aspects of supervision.

436. Stierlin, Helm; Rucker-Embden, Ingeborg; Wetzel, Norbert; and Wirsching, Michael. The First Interview with the Family. New York: Brunner/Mazel, Publisher, 1980. 239 pages.

This text presents a complete transcript of a first interview, with the authors' commentary, as well as numerous clinical vignettes. Also discussed are a number of practical considerations, such as the setting of the interview, use of audiovisual materials, and the presence of children. This text is appropriate for both the classroom and in-service training settings.

437. Suessmuth, Patrick. Ideals for Training Managers and Supervisors. San Diego, CA: University Associates Press, 1976. 328 pages.

This is a manual providing ready reference for use in management and supervisory training in the area of communication, leadership, decision making, and problem solving. This manual is adaptable to the human services organization for training supervisory personnel.

438. University of Michigan School of Social Work. A Learning Assessment Interview (Videocassette). University of Michigan Television Center, 400 Fourth Street, Ann Arbor, MI 48103, 1975. 9 minutes.

This videotape depicts a social worker and supervisor dealing with a job performance problem by defining the problem and discussing training options. The supervisor acts as a guide and facilitator.

439. University of Michigan School of Social Work. An Assessment Interview with Ruby Haynes (Videocassette). University of Michigan Television Center, 400 Fouth Street, Ann Arbor, MI 48103, 1975. 22 minutes.

This videotape is designed for training in family assessment. It presents the use of the family assessment interview and includes an interview with a client, Ruby Haynes. The client defines the problem and gives historical information, and talks about the reason referred to the agency. The worker discusses available resources to assist with problem resolution.

440. University of Michigan School of Social Work. An Assessment Interview with Sara Smith (Videocassette). University of Michigan Television Center, 400 Fourth Street, Ann Arbor, MI 48103, 1975. 27 minutes.

This videotape is designed for training in family assessment. It depicts a social worker interviewing

(University of Michigan)

an 18-year-old unmarried mother, Sara Smith, who allegedly has neglected her child. During the interview, the problems discussed are the family relationship involving mother and daughter and the extended family.

441. University of Michigan School of Social Work. Behavior Management: A Contracting Interview (Videocassettes). University of Michigan Television Center, 400 Fourth Street, Ann Arbor, MI 48130, 1975. 25 minutes.

This videotape depicts a social worker assisting her clients to negotiate a behavioral contract. The clients are a mother and daughter who have major concern over the daughter coming home late. The contract negotiated includes, among other things, a trade-off which allows the daughter to increase telephone usage for earlier hours in reporting home.

442. University of Michigan School of Social Work. Behavior Management: An Assessment Interview (Videocassettes). University of Michigan Television Center, 400 Fourth Street, Ann Arbor, MI 48103, 1975. 22 minutes.

This videotape illustrates a social worker interviewing a mother and her adolescent daughter about the problem of a strained relationship. The worker uses a behavior assessment interview approach and helps the clients define the problem and their feelings associated with it.

443. University of Michigan School of Social Work. Demonstration Tape (Videocassettes). University of Michigan Television Center, 400 Fourth Street, Ann Arbor, MI 48103, 1975. 32 minutes.

This videotape presents a social worker interviewing a client who is not ready to be engaged, It illustrates that shared decision-making is not a viable approach when the client will not participate.

444. University of Michigan School of Social Work. Lecture--Demonstration Tape (Videocassettes). University of Michigan Television Center, 400 Fourth Street, Ann Arbor, MI 48103, 1975. 25 minutes.

A social worker presents a lecture on the shared decision making process, which is nondirective and aids the client in identifying goals and the actions necessary for their achievement. The process is illustrated with a client interview.

445. University of Tennessee School of Social Work. Case Number 1 (Videocassette). Room 404, Andy Holt Tower, Knoxville, TN 37916, 1977. 60 minutes.

This videotape depicts an actual unrehearsed worker-client and worker-supervisor interview, accompanied by consultant critiques on the skills and techniques used. The worker-client interview is conducted on a multi-problem black family in an inner-city public housing project. The worker is white and middle-class and struggles with her value conflicts with the clients.

446. University of Tennessee School of Social Work. Case Number 2 (Videocassettes). Room 404, Andy Holt Tower, Knoxville, TN 37916, 1977. 60 minutes.

Two video materials are part of one training package. They present an actual unrehearsed worker-client and worker-supervisor interview, accompanied by consultant critiques on the skills and techniques employed. The case involves child abuse and neglect. The mother appears to be psychotic, thus giving the worker concern for the nine-year-old daughter recently returned to the mother from foster care.

447. University of Tennessee School of Social Work. Case Number 3 (Videocassettes). Room 404, Andy Holt Tower, Knoxville, TN 37916, 1977. 60 minutes.

This videotape presents an acutal unrehearsed worker-client and worker-supervisor interview, accompanied by consultant critiques on the skills and techniques used. The case involves child neglect. Through worker intervention, the mother's depression and father's heavy drinking subside and the couple begins to improve their communication.

448. University of Tennessee School of Social Work. Case Number 4 (Videocassettes). Room 404, Andy Holt Tower, Knoxville, TN 37916, 1977. 60 minutes.

This videotape presents an actual unrehearsed worker-client and worker-supervisor interview, accompanied by consultant critiques on the skills and techniques used. The case involves marital conflict and child neglect resulting in placement of two pre-school children. The mother moves to a different state, and the father remains and develops a service contract with the worker. The case illustrates the difficulty of working with one parent when the marital relationship is in flux.

449. University of Tennessee School of Social Work. Case Number 5 (Videocassettes). Room 404, Andy Holt Tower, Knoxville, TN 37916, 1977. 60 minutes.

This videotape presents an actual unrehearsed worker-client and worker-supervisor interview, accompanied by consultant critiques on the skills and techniques used. The case involves child neglect in an Appalachian social setting. The children involved have not been attending school. They are allowed to remain in the home if they attend school on a regular basis. The worker-client interview is conducted in the home and is intended to reinforce the judge's order.

450. University of Tennessee School of Social Work. Case Number 6 (Videocassettes). Room 404, Andy Holt Tower, Knoxville, TN 37916, 1977. 60 minutes.

This videotape presents an actual unrehearsed worker-client and worker-supervisor interview accompanied by consultant critiques on the skills and techniques used. The case involves child neglect of two small children. The mother has limited intelligence and is an excessive drinker. The worker-client interview illustrates the difficulties emerging from poor client engagement.

451. University of Tennessee School of Social Work. Case Number 7 (Videocassettes). Room 404, Andy Holt Tower, Knoxville, TN 37916, 1977. 60 minutes.

This videotape presents an actual unrehearsed worker-client interview and follow-up consultant critiques on the skills and techniques employed by the worker. The worker conducts an interview with parents whose children have been placed in foster care because of the parents' alcoholism. The father admits for the first time that alcoholism is contributing to family dysfunction and asks for help.

452. Wicks, Robert J. Counseling Strategies and Intervention Techniques for the Human Services. Philadelphia, PA: Lippincott Company, 1977. 159 pages.

This book begins with interviewing and covers the basic issues encountered in the interviewing process. Related topics covered deal with psychological testing, depression, anxiety and counseling.

453. Wilson, Suanna J. Recording Guidelines for Social Workers. New York: Macmillan Press, 1980. 241 pages.

This book is designed primarily for the teacher and beginning practitioner. It presents the primary concerns of social work recording. Much of the book is self-instructional. A section on diagnostic thinking presents an analytical thinking model that will be of interest to the more advanced practitioner. This book can be used for teaching principles of recording and basic interviewing skills to both supervisors and students.

AUTHOR INDEX

Including authors, joint authors and editors.
Numbers refer to individual entry number.

INDEX OF AUDIOVISUAL MATERIALS

This index lists alphabetically, by chapter, the published titles of audiovisual items. Numbers refer to individual entry number.

CHAPTER 1.

ABUSE AND NEGLECT

CHAPTER 2.

LAW AND THE COURT

CHAPTER 3.

SUBSTITUTE CARE

CHAPTER 4.

IN HOME SERVICE AND PARENT EDUCATION

CHAPTER 5.

INSTITUTIONS AND SPECIAL CHILDREN

CHAPTER 6.

MINORITY CLIENTS

CHAPTER 7.

TRAINING AND INTERVIEWING METHODS

SUBJECT INDEX

About the Compilers

JOHN T. PARDECK, Ph.D., is an Assistant Professor and Researcher in Social Work at Tulane University.

REBECCA L. HEGAR, M.S.S.W., is Coordinator of the Permanency Planning Project of the Region VI Child Welfare Center and is a Doctoral Candidate in Social Work at Tulane University.

KATHY NEWTON NANCE, M.S.S.W., Assistant Executive Director of Kingsley House and New Orleans Day Nursery Association, is currently enrolled in the O.S.W. program at Tulane University.

CYNTHIA CHRISTY-BAKER, M.S.N., currently serves as an Associate Research Fellow for Curriculum Development at Tulane University.